HEALING THE HU

FROM ISOLATIO

HEALING THE HURTS OF CAPITALISM

FROM ISOLATION TO CONNECTION

MICHELINE MASON AND ALAN SPRUNG

YOUCAXTON PUBLICATIONS

OXFORD & SHREWSBURY

CONTENTS

THE AUTHORS ARE GRATEFUL TO QUOTE FROM THE FOLLOWİNG:

'*Revolution*' by Russell Brand. Published by Century

'*The Human Side of Human Beings*' by Harvey Jackins. Published by Rational Island Publications

'*The Prophet*' by Kahlil Gibran

'*Evangelii Gaudium*' by Pope Francis

'*Snapshots of Possibility*' by The Alliance for Inclusive Education

'*To Have Or To Be*' by Erich Fromm. Published by Harper & Row

'*We Sell Everything*' by Leon Rosselson

'*The Case For Working With Your Hands*' by Matthew Crawford. Published by the Penguin Group

'*Stress and Psychological Disorders in Great Britain*' by the Health and Safety Executive

'*Trained to Kill*' by David Grossman. From Illuminati News

Section One

INTRODUCTION

WHO WE ARE

We are not the usual book-writing types and, on the face of it, we have nothing in common except our lack of qualifications, fame or notoriety and the fact that we were both born in 1950.

Alan is a man born in Coventry, in the Midlands of England, to a working class family. He was destined, like his Father, to work in the engineering industry in Coventry. Indeed, his early adulthood was spent working in engineering until boredom and restlessness moved him on.

Micheline is a woman, born near London where her early life was shaped by the experience of disability, keeping her corralled in the segregated world of 'special needs' and then as a trainee graphic illustrator, until boredom and restlessness moved her on.

We are two very different people bought together by our common desire to see a systemic, political change in the way we organise ourselves globally. We believe human life could be so much better than it is and that this better world is worth striving for.

OUR STARTING POINT – A MISSING PIECE OF THE PUZZLE

Many people are aware of all kinds of injustice, inequality, unfairness, oppression and general acts of inhumanity in this world, and are working hard to try to put these things right. In general many of us are good at envisioning a better world but we often seem 'booby-trapped' as if by a hidden emotional bomb, or mine, set to go off by the slightest provocation, and without warning, when we try to do something new, triggering unhelpful feelings and behaviours. Why is this?

It is apparent to anyone who is looking, that the ways we are forced to live in such an unequal world inflict varying degrees of emotional injuries on all of us. These injuries seem to impair our ability to treat each other humanely, and create these 'booby traps'. We believe that unless we find ways to 'de-activate' these booby traps, we run a serious risk of imposing old unworkable human relationships on any future enterprise we try. We will be pulled to sabotage our own dreams. The book offers an explanation as to why this happens, and a way to begin a process which empowers us to help each other to recover from these emotional injuries, freeing us to find new and creative ways to build the world we really want.

The Problem is Systemic, not Personal

"There is nothing wrong with anyone except the effects of their mistreatment" **Harvey Jackins**[1]

Capitalism is the dominating world economic system and it causes much more damage to people and the natural world than is commonly recognised. Obvious examples are war, the effects of poverty, industrial accidents, pollution, extinction of species and global warming. All of this damage also leaves an emotional legacy of hurt e.g. grief, fear, confusion and internalised violence.

There is increasing disquiet with the growing inequality of power and wealth between the one percent and the ninety-nine percent, and increasing resentment towards bankers and corporate bosses who we blame for this, but there needs to be a distinction made between

---

1   Harvey Jackins was a political activist in the USA. He founded the International Re-Evaluation Co-Counseling Community.

the people who are coerced to play all the different oppressive roles within the system and the system itself.

A commonly held view is that this inequality reflects the fact that there are simply good people like 'us', and bad people like 'them'. We are expected to continually judge who is which, to side with the 'good' ones and try to beat, change, ignore, punish, threaten or even eliminate the 'bad' ones. We often notice that these attempts do not work, but we plough on regardless, doing the same things only more so, confused by the fact that the problem only gets worse. The 'War on Terror' (with its attempt to beat violence with greater violence) is a current example of this. Our explanation for this is different to most commonly held views. What we both have come to understand is that there has been a missing piece of information about human behaviour that challenges this view fundamentally:

Under capitalism (as with all oppressive systems) we get hurt. These hurts, which are felt in some way by everyone – losers and 'winners' – are a direct result of being raised and living under this system. Unhealed, they install patterns of distressed behaviour that have the effect of temporarily shutting down our usual intelligence and replacing it with rigid and repetitive behaviours when we are in situations that remind us enough of our early hurtful experiences.

We might be in a group of people for example, where we want to say something, but once there find we are reminded of being at school. Depending on our experience of school this might just be an interesting memory, or it might make our internal 'booby trap' explode, rendering us suddenly completely tongue-tied out of fear of humiliation, as if we were still back there.

Or there might be a knock at the door to which we relaxedly go to answer until we see through the glass that it is the police wanting to speak to us. Suddenly we are flooded with fear – "Who had died?", "What has my son done now?", "What have I done wrong?" – all assumptions based on past negative information or experiences. We might almost fall over with relief when they announce that they have found the wallet that we dropped that morning when going to buy the milk. This strange debilitating process has been called 'restimulation', or 'having our buttons pushed'.

This phenomenon severely hampers us when trying to do something in a new way. However different we want our creations to be, we are constantly pulled by our 'buttons' to act in ways that we learned from the past. Soon we find we have re-created the past complete with all its problems instead. We gather people together around a beautiful vision of peace, but start fighting and arguing with each other, creating hierarchies, competing and excluding, gossiping and being rude to each other on Facebook. We unawarely act out learned, oppressive attitudes and behaviours towards each other and forget things like the fact that wheelchair users cannot climb stairs and vegetarians don't eat meat. We wonder why no one comes to our meetings except the three people who are just like us, and blame it on the apathy of other people. The organised Left in Britain and many other liberation movements around the world are notorious for ignoring the ninety-nine things they have agreement over and splitting up over the one thing which they don't.

At their most extreme these 'patterns' and our vulnerability to restimulation, can make us very dangerous, able to abuse and kill others without guilt or remorse.

Without understanding this phenomenon, much of what we people do is incomprehensible but, once understood, it becomes something we can recognise and learn to deal with. Instead of launching into conflicts, our approach becomes 'What help does this person need in order to heal whatever hurts led them to behave in such undesirable ways?' Alan recounts a story from his own experience that may serve as an example of this different approach:

Alan: "Some time ago, I was lying in bed. It was about eleven o'clock on a Friday night. I was just going to sleep and. outside my bedroom window, I heard an argument between a young man and a young woman – essentially, the young man was giving the young woman a hard time about something. I couldn't hear all the details but I could hear his aggressive tone of voice.

As I lay there listening, it sounded like the situation was escalating and I then started to debate in my mind whether I was going to get out of bed nd try to sort out what was going on.

As I lay there, I was battling my fears about going out and confronting somebody who I couldn't even see. I hadn't looked out of the window at that point so I was a bit nervous about doing it at all but, after a short while, I made the decision to go and sort it out so I threw some clothes on and went outside to discover this young man, standing in the middle of the road, haranguing his girlfriend. He was doing all the shouting. She wasn't saying a great deal at all.

I went over to them and I initially put myself between him and her, at which point he, of course, turned his attention to me. He said something like, 'This is between me and my girlfriend. Don't you start interfering!'

I remember saying to him that my name was Alan, that I lived at the house on the corner and that I didn't want to do him any harm.

By this time I'd realised that he didn't look like he would be a physical threat to me so I wasn't so scared – he didn't look so big and terrifying as he'd seemed when I was lying in bed. That made it easier for me. I was still feeling scared. I remember that my legs were shaking because there was still some degree of physical threat and, anyway, I wasn't at all sure what I was going to be able to do that would be useful.

I think I said something like, 'It looks like you're having some kind of difficulty. Maybe I can help.'

I don't remember in detail everything that was said or that happened but the main thing I remember was that I was keeping my attention on him. I didn't pay very much attention to what his girlfriend was doing, in fact I had my back to her most of the time.

While I was trying to talk to the young man, two women appeared at the doorway of a nearby house and they started to shout at him about the fact that he was giving his girlfriend a hard time and then they started haranguing his girlfriend, 'Why do you put up with that kind of behaviour from your boyfriend?' This was just escalating the situation.

Somehow I managed to usher the young man to the pavement on the side of the road and he stood leaning against a wall as I was trying to discover what was going on – I was interested in what was troubling him.

He didn't say anything – he just went quiet. I was simply staying with him trying to be helpful when two young guys appeared from down the street and one of them, very quickly, produced a big carving knife and proceeded to threaten the young man with what they were going to do to him if he didn't stop mistreating his girlfriend!

I then found myself in the position of having to protect the young man from these two guys and their knife! The knife obviously wasn't going to do anybody any good so I then found myself between the carving knife and the guy I was trying to help!

I remember saying to these two young lads, 'Look lads, that's not going to help' and I told them they should go back to their house and leave me to sort it out which, luckily, they did.

When they'd moved away and I turned my attention back to the young man he started to cry. He still didn't say anything but maybe he understood that I was for real – that I really did want to help and that I'd protected him from the two characters with the knife.

He had clearly been drinking so he wasn't thinking very straight and still he said nothing at all. He shed a few tears but then he just went over to a car and drove off.

So, I had no idea who he was or where he went and I never heard any more about him. By this time his girlfriend had disappeared – I think she probably lived nearby and she'd gone off."

Micheline: *"What made you get out of bed?"*

Alan: *"It sounded like the threat from the young man, who'd obviously been drinking, to the young woman was escalating to a dangerous* *level. I could tell from the tone in his voice and I didn't want her to get any more hurt than she obviously already had been! So, I guess I got out of bed in her defence."*

Micheline: *"But you got out of bed with no guns or knives or weapons or anything so you must have thought, 'I can do something about this without them'. There must have been something in you that felt you could intervene in a useful way."*

Alan: *"It just seemed clear where the problem was and that he needed a hand – a friendly hand – from someone who was going to be a bit thoughtful around him and his struggle, rather than giving him a hard time or beating him up or whatever."*

As can be seen from this example these hurts do not just leave a legacy on the victims of such injuries, but also on the perpetrators. Any system which compels us to act in ways which are harmful to ourselves or each other is inflicting a 'hurt' on everyone involved. Perpetrators are often left with feelings of great shame, denial, numbness and other behaviours which compromise their humanity.

How Did We Humans Get Here?

We can only guess at how we have become loaded down with accumulated distress patterns and why they have taken the form they have.

Sometime during the early days of human habitation of every type of environment on this planet – in the rain forests, the deserts, the frozen lands, the grassy planes, beside rivers and oceans and in the high mountains – we realised that living in social groups was, on balance, far more beneficial to our survival than living alone. We could work together to locate food and water, we could provide more substantial shelters, we could defend ourselves from attack, we could work together to achieve common goals and, crucially, we could learn from each other's experiences.

It seems that during that chapter of our human story we were nomadic, hunter-gatherers. In those early days, our hand tools were very basic and we were forced to travel to fulfill our fundamental needs for water, food and shelter. Our species survived but our lives were short and life was tough.

Over a long period of time, we slowly managed to improve our tools, we learned about the advantages of keeping and breeding animals and we figured out some things about planting seeds and harvesting and storing crops. We reached a stage in our development, having improved our tools and learned how to feed ourselves more efficiently, where we were able to produce more food than we needed for our basic survival – we developed the capacity to produce a *surplus*.

This was a critically important moment in the history of our species because it was at this point that some very important questions arose concerning how we should make use of this surplus. Should we put the surplus to some collective good or should the fittest and strongest amongst us, who had physically produced more of the surplus, keep a bigger share for themselves – for the benefit of themselves and their families?

Because of our earlier experiences of threats to our survival, over many generations, we were still very fearful for our own survival and this made it difficult to arrive at rational answers to questions about the surplus or to arrive at answers by consensus. When we humans are feeling afraid we don't think or act rationally, we can become greedy, self-interested, dominating, arrogant, aggressive, and, in so doing, we isolate ourselves from others.

Since that point in human history, when we developed the capability to produce surplus, we have made huge progress in our ability to meet our inherent needs to feed, clothe and shelter ourselves. We have utilised our amazing intelligence to consistently improve our capacity to make progress on almost every front of human endeavor: purifying water, growing an abundance of food and creating comfortable living spaces in any kind of adverse environment – including the vacuum through which we move during space exploration.

So, as a species, we far exceed our capacity to not only sustain ourselves but to enhance our many and varied cultural pursuits. However, the old fears about whether we can find enough of the necessities of life for our survival persist to this day. These fears still have the power to over-ride our rational behaviour and when they do, when we are in the grips of these feelings, we can act in ways which are inhuman, such as hoarding enormous wealth whilst others starve, or dropping nuclear bombs on innocent people.

THE NEXT ECONOMY

The current 'for-profit' system cannot be reformed. It must be replaced – not in a bloody revolution sort of way but in an intelligent, compassionate and creative sort of way.

Capitalism is by nature an exploitative, competitive and cut-throat system. It is concerned with only one central and overriding issue – how to make and accumulate wealth for the benefit of a shrinking number of owners and shareholders of companies, corporations and other financial institutions.

> *"According to Ol' Piketty ('Capital in the 21st Century' – Thomas Piketty 2014) our system, capitalism, is designed to behave like this: it generates wealth for the wealthy and further impoverishes those with nothing. Asking it to behave differently is like asking a microwave to wash your car."* **Russell Brand, 'Revolution'**

Whether we blame the stark economic inequalities which we see in our societies on the laziness of the poor or the greed of the rich, we are still missing the point – rather than being an unintended by-product, they are a direct result and consequences of the system itself. This is deeply confusing to people and it is meant to be.

As its true nature becomes more and more obvious and extreme, many people, from all walks of life, are beginning to ring the alarm bells:

> *"Almost half of the world's wealth is now owned by just one percent of the population, and seven out of ten people live in countries where economic inequality has increased in the last 30 years. The World Economic Forum has identified economic inequality as a major risk to human progress, impacting social stability within countries and threatening security on a global scale. This massive concentration of economic resources in the hands of fewer people presents a real threat to inclusive political and economic systems, and compounds other inequalities – such as those between women and men. Left unchecked, political institutions are undermined and governments overwhelmingly serve the interests of economic elites – to the detriment of ordinary people"* **Working for the Few: Political Capture & Economic Inequality, Oxfam 2014**

Even the current Pope has been speaking out against the workings of the system. In an 84-page *Evangelii Gaudium* (Joy of the Gospel), Pope Francis issued harsh judgement of neoliberal, 21st century capitalism:

> *"Just as the commandment "Thou shalt not kill" sets a clear limit in order to safeguard the value of human life, today we also have to say "thou shalt not" to an economy of exclusion and inequality. Such an economy kills. How can it be that it is not a news item when an elderly homeless person dies of exposure, but it is news when the stock market loses two points? This is a case of exclusion. Can we continue to stand by when food is thrown away while people are starving? This is a case of inequality. Today everything comes under the laws of competition and the survival of the fittest, where the powerful feed upon the powerless. As a consequence, masses of*

people find themselves excluded and marginalized: without work, without possibilities, without any means of escape.

Human beings are themselves considered consumer goods to be used and then discarded. We have created a "throw away" culture which is now spreading. It is no longer simply about exploitation and oppression, but something new. Exclusion ultimately has to do with what it means to be a part of the society in which we live; those excluded are no longer society's underside or its fringes or its disenfranchised – they are no longer even a part of it. The excluded are not the "exploited" but the outcast, the "leftovers".

In this context, some people continue to defend trickle-down theories which assume that economic growth, encouraged by a free market, will inevitably succeed in bringing about greater justice and inclusiveness in the world. This opinion, which has never been confirmed by the facts, expresses a crude and naïve trust in the goodness of those wielding economic power and in the sacralized workings of the prevailing economic system. Meanwhile, the excluded are still waiting. To sustain a lifestyle which excludes others, or to sustain enthusiasm for that selfish ideal, a globalization of indifference has developed. Almost without being aware of it, we end up being incapable of feeling compassion at the outcry of the poor, weeping for other people's pain, and feeling a need to help them, as though all this were someone else's responsibility and not our own. The culture of prosperity deadens us; we are thrilled if the market offers us something new to purchase. In the meantime all those lives stunted for lack of opportunity seem a mere spectacle; they fail to move us". **Pope Francis 2014, Evangelii Gaudium, Chapter Two, paragraphs 52 – 54**

THE CURRENT DILEMMA

There is no shortage of good thinking about possible ways forward for human beings and the natural world upon which we depend.

Around every problem of which we are currently aware, people have got together to think of solutions, and to try things out. For example:

- The poor agricultural workers of the world have already organised in their millions through 'Via Compesina'[2] (from the Spanish 'la vía campesina', meaning 'the peasants' way') and were the first to develop the concept of 'food sovereignty'. Food sovereignty refers to the right to prioritise the production of food to feed your own population from one's own territory over the use of land to produce cash crops for export.

- The co-operative movement has already created working models such as Mondragon in the Basque Country which addresses the problem of profit-sharing, worker ownership, co-operation and has shown it has the ability to survive whilst capitalism collapses around it.

- The environmental movement has already put the seed of every known living plant into safe keeping, learned how to bring back desperately threatened creatures from near extinction, fought for and begun to legislate for areas of land and ocean to be set aside for the regeneration of endangered bird, animal and fish species, especially those we hunt and eat. It is also beginning to develop the technology to harness the abundance of sustainable energy from the wind, waves and sun on a scale which could eventually replace our harmful use of fossil fuels or nuclear power.

- The Co-Housing Movement has already set up communities of people who choose to live together in a balance of individual and shared living spaces, managed collectively. Denmark, for

---

2   For more information, see http://en.wikipedia.org/wiki/Via_Campesina

instance, has 8% of its population living in such schemes which have been proven to help people live longer, happier lives, and to be more ecologically sound than when living in traditional housing in the industrialised world.

- Health workers around the world have already worked together to eliminate infectious diseases, such as smallpox, from the planet, partially eradicated many others and developed treatments for many injuries and diseases which would once have left people in life-long pain and suffering. For example, surgeons with skill around cleft palates and hare lips – congenital conditions which have relegated many children and adults to a lifetime of struggle around eating and speaking – can now stitch them up so they are no longer a problem to the child.

- The inclusion movement is already learning how to create inclusive communities, especially for children, where emotional, physical or intellectual needs are met on an individualised basis but within the heart of young people's schools and communities. Friendship is seen as an educational goal and children, who were once separated by the fears and prejudices of adults, are able to make connections, learn about differences and, more importantly, discover the overriding *commonalities* they have as human beings.

Of course, our current best efforts are constrained by having to survive within the capitalist system. For example, competition for funding between voluntary organisations means that they are turned into rivals, which then makes it difficult to collaborate. Co-ops still have to survive in the global market place. Capitalism is the major creator of ill-health (through poverty, wars, exploitation at work, addictions, stress etc) and it is not possible to bring about true inclusion within a system designed for the benefit of capital.

We cannot foresee in detail what the future will look like when the current collapsing economic system is replaced. However, the long history of voluntary, not-for-profit organisations, unions and campaigns which engage enthusiasts and experts in their tens of thousands to focus on particular social issues has already created enough expertise that, were it pooled and acted upon on a large enough scale, would make the world a much better place, even whilst the economic system is in a state of transition. Such models would also create the conditions of security and safety which we need in order for our full creativity and long-term problem-solving abilities to flourish.

So the problem is not that we don't know what to do. It is not that we don't have working examples of progressive practices. It is not that we don't have our arguments finely tuned enough or well-researched enough or delivered in enough of an authoritarian tone. We have filled our libraries and lecture halls with enough learned papers and PowerPoint presentations to sink an island. The problem is that **we just don't do it**.

Many of us wake up every morning, knowing at some level that we are living in a time-limited and irrational system. We feel that it becomes more of a struggle to survive financially on a daily basis. We are bored, tired, afraid for our children and for our own future when we get old and decrepit. Yet we get dressed and gobble up some sort of breakfast, feeling we have no choice but to just get on with it. We hurry our children off to school, hurry to work, hurry to get the shopping, do our chores, pay our bills, cook the meals, clean up things and people, flop in front of the TV getting depressed at the 'News' until it is time to drag ourselves to bed in order to sleep, in order to get up the next morning and start all over again – or variations on this theme with the addition of sex and drugs.

Sometimes we do turn out on the streets with carefully crafted placards, drums and megaphones, with thousands of others, to protest about the latest atrocity our government is doing in our name. We march and shout, bang our drums, gather in Hyde Park or equivalent meeting place, cheer our speakers, eat our sandwiches, gather a few hugs and kisses from dusty comrades and then go home in the full expectation of being ignored. In the morning we get up, sigh and prop up the system again by putting our shoulder back to the grindstone. But at least our conscience is soothed a little by knowing we said we disagreed as we try not to think about all those dead children.

Or, we do decide to be an activist, to try and do something about our beliefs, religious or political, but we cannot find the 'right' people to do it with. They don't think quite like we do and they become annoying or we annoy them or the council won't listen or other people don't pull their weight or we don't find the time to go to the meetings or Dad is ill and needs us and anyway the funding runs out. Our beautiful progressive movement becomes factionalised and dragged down by in-fighting until disillusionment and exhaustion set in and make it ineffective.

Why is this?

KEY UNIVERSAL HURTS

Some of the hurts that we believe are hampering us are: isolation, competition, materialism, oppression, including its internalised form, the exploitation of labour (paid and unpaid), addictions and violence – all of which are learned rather than inborn.

It has been our experience that when we start to acknowledge and heal these hurts, we begin to change. We develop:

- More of a sense of connection and empathy with other people and nature;

- A desire to do work which is meaningful to us and for the common good;

- A recovery from addictions of all kinds;

- Less reliance on shopping or possessions to feel good about ourselves, or to feel secure;

- A good sense of the difference between our status and our worth;

- A hunger to learn about people who appear 'different' from us;

- A distaste for violence and

- A growing fundamental attitude of loving protectiveness towards the world and all its' wonders, including ourselves.

> *"As soon as someone pipes up with 'There ain't no climate change' or 'Compassionate Capitalism could work' we should just nod, smile and lead them to the sanatorium to begin their re-education. Redemption is possible and compassion a prerequisite. If we don't allow people to change, then how can we change the world?"* **Russell Brand**

Can we help each other to heal from these hurts – to really change?

SETTING UP THE WORKSHOPS

We know from our own experience that the 'simple' act of creating a space in which people can speak aloud without interruption or judgement can start-up this healing process. Therefore part of the exploration we undertook for this book was to see what would happen if we set up structured meetings in which people were given the opportunity to think aloud with the attention of others. We also wanted to see whether the usefulness of these spaces could be intensified by asking people to think about really challenging questions e.g. 'What were your first memories around violence?'

With all this in mind, we decided to run a series of small, experimental workshops, each one focused on one of the areas of 'hurt' that we had identified. It was our hope that this safe space would furnish us with some 'straight-from-the-horse's-mouth' examples that would illustrate both the nature of the problem and point towards part of the solution. We thought a lot about how to run the workshops in ways that would benefit us as we researched this book but that would also benefit the participants whom we were asking to bare their souls in front of strangers. We had to work this out before we sent out our invitations.

The participants were all personally invited friends or acquaintances who we thought might be interested and who would have something to say on the issue. We noted, however, that it was mostly our closer friends – the ones who had a degree of trust in us – who were actually brave enough to turn up.

We chose people from as wide a diversity as we could – bearing in mind, age, class background, ethnicity and religious identity in particular. The experience of running these mixed identity workshops, however, led us to run two single identity workshops to make it safer for them. These were for people who were 'raised poor' and for 'young adults' (between eighteen and thirty years of age).

The workshops' participants were small in number ranging from six to ten people – including ourselves. Most were held in private homes and we tried to organise them around the country.

The formula we decided upon seemed to work well with all the groups, with minor variations that we will describe.

BUILDING THE SAFETY

We divided each day into two halves with lunch in the middle. The morning sessions looked at the 'hurts', e.g. 'isolation' whilst the afternoon sessions looked at how we could help each other move forward in a more human direction, e.g. 'connection'.

As we believe that music can help move us from our everyday concerns to a deeper place, we began many of the sections with a song – chosen and sometimes written and sung by Alan. We also prepared a short introduction to both our method of working and the subject itself.

Posing the Questions

We thought very carefully about the questions we asked. Most of our distress patterns are first set in place when we are children. The early hurts form the 'sticky floor' to which later, similar events glue themselves. It is useful to try to clean the sticky floor by retracing our current painful feelings to the first time we remember feeling them. This seems to speed up the healing process and is why we started by thinking about our early lives. All the workshops began with asking people about their earliest memories connected with the subject e.g. "What are you first memories to do with competition?"

The time we had allocated was divided into three to six minute slots and regulated with a timer which peeped as each person's time came to an end. For the duration of each person's time, no one else was allowed to butt in, criticise, comment or disagree. Although there was a general discussion at the end, no one was allowed to refer to what had been said in the timed spots. What they had said was to be considered confidential to the person unless they themselves wanted to bring it up later. This allowed people to share some very personal and sometimes 'raw' memories.

The afternoon sessions also began with a song and an introduction. We attempted to help people look at how these early experiences still impact on our lives and affect our behaviour now. We encouraged as much emotional expression – laughter, tears, anger as came up whilst people were talking, although this was limited by the short time available.

Variations

The young people's workshop was slightly different. It was not on a particular subject, as we wanted their perspective on everything. Instead, we asked one main question divided into two – "How has capitalism impacted on your family?" and "How has capitalism impacted on you?" The responses were so rich there was no need to ask any other questions. The discussion about addictions was particularly useful.

In the workshop for people who were raised in relative poverty, which was on the subject of work, we added an exercise which involved physically moving around and creating visual wall charts:

We put up two large sheets of paper, one headed 'Necessary Work' and the other headed 'Work for Profit'. Each person was given a few post-it notes upon which was written a wide variety of jobs or professions. They were asked to assign each post-it to one or other of the headed sheets. They were also asked to write down their own main area of work on a blank note and post that up also. We then stood back and looked at the picture that had emerged.

Most, if not all, the work considered necessary was low-paid or voluntary, including our public services, food production and preparation, parenting, caring for sick or elderly people, providing emotional support to people in crisis, 'housework' and even gardening.

Most, if not all, the work on the 'Work For Profit' sheet were engaged in production of luxury goods and services, celebrity, making money from people's addictions, sports stars, financial services and academia.

It took some discussion to understand that we can and do provide public goods and services without needing to make a profit. Most importantly perhaps, we could see in graphic detail from the sheets of paper that the system as a whole could not function without the massive input, mostly from women, of unpaid labour – cooking, shopping, childcare, cleaning and maintenance of our living spaces, bed making, laundry, care of people in need, all kinds of voluntary work (e.g. grandparents provide over half of all child care to working parents for free). This is often thought of and described, in society at large, as 'doing nothing'.

We made an attempt to create our own chart showing what makes work meaningful and how it should be valued, which, not surprisingly, was almost the diametric opposite of this picture. We put people who care for others at the top of the list, with arms traders near the bottom.

This process led to new insights for people taking part and taught us something about how to facilitate the thinking of non-academics and people with little confidence in 'speaking out'.

We both took part as peers in the timed sessions. What was interesting to note was that, with the attention of the group, we ourselves were facilitated to remember and describe bits of our personal histories which were not so accessible when we were alone. We have added these bits into the text as quotes, alongside everyone else's, to separate them from the main body of text that came from a different place in our minds.

CLOSING ROUND

We ended each workshop with a round of feedback about the process we had used which, for the most part, people found stimulating and useful. (See the Conclusion on page 149).

For the first workshop we relied on notes to record what people said but quickly realised this was inadequate. We invested in a digital recorder and used it in all others – despite the tedious slog of transcribing everything. It was amazing listening back to the recordings to hear the many details we had not heard the first time – or had forgotten.

When it came to writing the book, the material we had gathered did not fit so neatly as we thought under each subject heading. Many contributions were good illustrations to other issues, so the finished article has everyone's voices scattered throughout.

What follows is based on what came out of these workshops laced together with our own thinking, further interviews and wider research. We hope it will encourage you, the reader, to look again at yourself, your families, your comrades and world affairs from a different angle. We see it as a framework from which to hang your own experiences, thoughts and questions so these ideas get developed much further.

Section Two
The Workshops

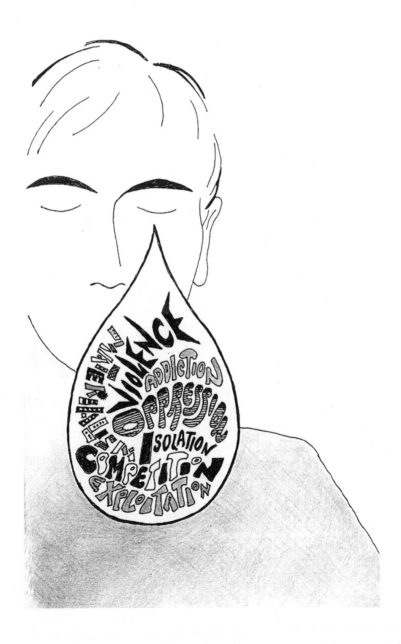

From Isolation to Connection

We are not like the male polar bear. He is a lone hunter padding across the ice for most of the year, only seeking out another bear for a few days a year to mate and then drifting off again into the cold and sparse surroundings. Humans have instead evolved over hundreds of thousands of years as tribal animals. Our survival has depended on it. Isolation is neither beneficial nor natural to us. Solitary confinement is one of the worst punishments we can dream up because we acknowledge that to deprive one another of human company is enormously hurtful and frightening. It could be said that it is against our human nature.

Yet, in a world with a population of 9 billion people, it is possible for most of us to drift through life feeling pretty much on our own, especially those of us in the so called 'developed' world. How has this come about? And why?

There are many ways we are made to become disconnected and isolated, most of which are unintentional by-products of the system in which we live but they are, nevertheless, useful to it – but not to us.

It probably started at birth, when we lost our safe haven of a womb and entered the world full of its wonders and weirdnesses, totally vulnerable and dependent on the attention of the first humans with whom we came into contact. This could have been an unpredictable and varied experience ranging from a softly lit birthing room where a skilled and gentle midwife eased your passage onto the waiting warm skin of your delighted mother who cooed and cried with joy as you suckled her sweet perfect milk, to a slap on the bottom and a grunt of disappointment as it was observed that the little things between your legs were not the ones hoped for.

Babies in the past and still, in some of the poorer parts of the world, spend most of their first few years next to their mothers, tied on their back as they work or running around with other children in the open houses and courtyards of the village. Many were breast-fed for years not months.

However, as capitalism progresses in its take-over around the world, the way of life which made this possible, living rurally and sustainably off the land, becomes threatened by industrialisation. Children of poor families may have to suffer the loss of their fathers or even mothers too – forced to move away into the town or city or abroad, to earn enough money to feed the family, in factories or as domestic servants.

This was just as true for the working class in England as it was in any other country. In fact, the English were the first to industrialise and the first to have their lands enclosed and must therefore have been the first to suffer this huge displacement from the land to the city with the consequent loss of their traditional culture of constant closeness with suckling infants and children.

So, it is likely that we have habituated ourselves to a level of separation right from the start – which is not what babies really need! Weird child development theories written by professionals such as the infamous Dr Spock who told parents to only feed their babies once every four hours and to ignore their cries of hunger until the clock hands said the 'right' time. He did much to make things worse. The culture, which encouraged parents not to sleep in the same bed with their newly born infants but to put them, not just in a cot, but *in another room,* added to the trend.

Some of us can remember being put outside in the fresh air to sleep when we were still a tiny baby in a pram – sometime right at the bottom of the garden or in the shed. This was also considered a good thing by the professionals. The idea was to stop you controlling your parents by 'attention seeking' behaviours (such as howling with hunger pains). We are only just beginning to understand how this lack of response to our cries for our mothers leads us to feel alone and powerless – sometimes for the rest of our lives.

A mother's breasts produce milk when she hears her infant's cry of hunger. Her mind and body is designed to respond to the child's voice, so it is likely that it is also a 'hurt' to the mother to force herself to ignore her babies cues. She must learn to 'stop listening' to some degree and it is logical to think that this will become a 'pattern' throughout the child's life. A disconnection has begun which may be hard to end.

Once, as infants, we are disconnected to some degree from our own power to call for attention and from the natural response of our primary care-givers, including both mothers and fathers, we probably have the foundation for the many other attacks on our sense of connection which come on a daily basis from the adult world.

The threat of isolation is often used to control children by fear:

Tara: "As a child in my 'special' school I can remember watching other children being sent to bed at six o'clock without any supper because they had been 'too slow' getting to the dining hall. I was so upset that I really struggled to eat my own tea whilst I knew this was happening".

Most of us in industrialised countries were brought up in 'nuclear families', not within the wider communities of extended family and tribe or clan members. A growing number of children grow up with just one adult, living an isolated life in a tower block or some such compartmentalised housing stock. Visitors are few, other family members not necessarily nearby, nowhere safe to play outside, doors locked, television on, and no one to witness whatever happens inside.

All levels of society create their own forms of separation and disconnection from others 'not like us'. Children in nuclear families are usually only able to mix with other children like them – same ethnicity, same class, same language, same cultures:

Zelda: "*I grew up as a Jew in New York surrounded only by other Jews. It was never spoken about and I thought it was normal. It was only when we went on holiday with gentiles present that I remember my Dad saying '"Oh, they are alright really.'"*

We are only allowed by our families to play with certain children, and our school is often chosen on the basis of a 'peer group' defined by our parents' aspirations, most apparent in the practice of the monied classes of putting their child's name down for a prestigious private school before they are even out of nappies.

In this way every group comes to feel that we are the 'normal' ones and everyone else isn't:

Micheline: "*I can remember thinking how strange it was when someone (from Yorkshire I think) referred to my London 'accent' when it was obvious to me that I spoke normally and only other people had accents.*"

When you are taught that you are the normal one(s) and you cannot verify this by real interaction with 'others', then it is easy to become prejudiced, scared and alienated from them. This, of course, feeds many of the other difficulties associated with capitalism, such as racism, classism and war.

Because this relationship is fundamental to our survival, considerable force may be needed to break the connection between family members, particularly parents and their children:

Jennifer D: "*Every day of my life I have to push through the world's judgements and attempts to disconnect me from my own daughter because she has learning difficulties. It started before she was born, with a routine ultra-sound screening test."*

David: *"My sister was institutionalised the day before I was born. I didn't know her then. Even when my parents were visiting her, I was left outside in the car because they thought I wouldn't like it. Eventually visits stopped but I remember that the connection between my Mum and her never died. I watched her knit her a new bed-jacket every Christmas."*

The education system is the capitalist's sorting ground. In it we are all groomed for particular roles in the adult world – whichever roles are currently needed by the requirements of the economic system. Even though all children in the UK supposedly have equal rights to a free and full-time education from age three to eighteen, with a '... broad and balanced curriculum, aimed to promote pupils' spiritual, moral, social and cultural development and prepare all pupils for the opportunities, responsibilities and experiences of life' (1944 Education Act), the reality is very much less 'equal'.

Whilst parents still have a legal right to choose to educate their children at home with the support of organisations such as 'Education Otherwise', this is not a practical proposition for the vast majority of us. Therefore most children are educated in schools.

There are already many different types of school for different 'types' of children, and this number seems to be increasing daily. They include mainstream nursery, primary and secondary schools, single sex schools, faith schools, comprehensive schools, grammar schools, free schools, academies, several different kinds of 'special' schools, Human Scale schools, boarding schools, private schools and specialist independent schools such as Steiner or Montessori schools, supplemented by home tuition, pupil referral units, detention centres, youth offender units and 'lock-ups'.

What the majority of us experience in any of these schools is the fear of being different – being excluded from our peer group – and the enormous power this has on our desire to conform or, conversely, on our unwillingness to stand out from the crowd, despite what we may feel inside. Being cool at school is *survival*. This can affect who you choose as your friends:

Jennifer D: *"There was one black child in my school and I made friends with him. I remember announcing this one dinner time and the whole room went quiet. It was not the right thing to do!"*.

Ella: *"I was friends with Ahmed when I was about seven. We had fun together but it was considered strange for a girl to be friends and playmates with a boy. I did not even notice he was from an ethnic background different to myself. It wasn't an issue then."*

The hurts installed in us by the arbitrary divisions set up at school and continued into higher education can create long-term difficulties. Will talks about his struggle to re-connect with the friends he had before he went to university:

Will: *"There was a time when my only topic of conversation was 'what is wrong with the world' and how to put it right. I was very intense. I drifted away from my other friends who wanted to talk about cars and football. I thought they were superficial but now I miss them. I realize all of our different ways of connecting are important."*

Being labeled as 'not clever enough' brings with it the real fear of being removed from your peer group in order to let them speed ahead:

Jackie: *"It still upsets me to remember the day when I was called out of the class at my mainstream school. I was about seven. There was a man in a suit who didn't know me. I had never seen him before. He gave me tests I had never seen and that day his judgements shattered my life. He met me for one day and didn't*

even say goodbye. He said I had to go to a special school after that.
Where are your human rights in that? I felt stupid, backward,
like an idiot with no sense. I was ashamed. Everyone else I knew
went to a proper school."[3]

As we are separated and individualized, the whole concept of
community is becoming a thing of the past. If you are excluded
from the paid labour force, you are virtually excluded from life itself.

People who have retired are also often increasingly vulnerable to
isolation as close relatives may have moved away, may be too busy or
may themselves be of an age where they have their own support needs.
The company once enjoyed through public services such as older
people's luncheon clubs has fallen victim to the 'austerity' measures
as has the delivery of hot meals by human beings:

"A new study has found that more than a million over 65s have
described themselves as lonely and have not spoken to anyone in
a month. Two in five state their TV or pet is their main form of
company." **Age UK, May 2012**

The British owning class has perfected the process of isolation and
disconnection for their children – having been brought up themselves
to believe it to be a necessary precursor to being able to stand alone
and take charge in later life. Many owning class adults speak with great
emotion about the relationships they had with their nannies when very
young – people who, though paid to look after them, still offered the most
physical warmth and affection such children may have ever experienced.

Whatever class you come from, most of us had parents who were
not prepared particularly well to deal with newborn babies. Because

---

3   From 'Dear Parents' by Micheline Mason, published by www.
inclusive-solutions.com.

of all the pressures on their lives and because of the 'baggage' they carry about parenting, babies and responsibility, few of us get the most thoughtful and warm welcome into this world that we all deserve. Because, as newborn babies, we are all physically and emotionally reliant on the adults around us to meet our every need, which doesn't always go smoothly, we are often left isolated and struggling with the thoughtlessness, or shortcomings of those around us.

It's not difficult to see how young ones, exposed to enough of this unawareness, could end up losing their sense of hopefulness about ever being closely connected to other human beings acting thoughtfully towards them.

When we get a little older and we're still struggling with having close and meaningful connections with other people, society presents us with sex and romance, which is billed as our great ticket to closeness and connection. We, of course, in our desperation, jump at it!

Our problem is that by this time we've all got so many hang-ups and confusions about sex and real human connection that we can't imagine real closeness and intimacy outside of a sexual relationship.

Many of us (in the West) grew up being told that there was just one other person out there who could and would answer all our needs for attention, closeness and love – if only we could find them! We would marry them and live happily ever after.

Of course, there are markets to be exploited in helping people in this quest for their perfect partner. The glamour industry is just one. When our need to find someone to love us is overlaid with the idea that the search is a competition we must win or else be lonely all our lives, then there is no end to the things we can be sold to help us beat the competition – cosmetics, clothes, jewelry, perfumes and after shaves, body building and diets, hair dos and even cosmetic surgery. There are songs, films, books, magazines, cards, bunches of flowers, dating agencies and so on stretching far into the rosy-pink distance.

Sadly, the highly-charged nature of these relationships with their huge expectations, as we all know, can also be intense channels for disappointment, jealousy and abuse. Our sexuality is also vulnerable to becoming distorted by our distresses, including addictions. Pornographic websites, for example, are the sites most visited by men.

Nevertheless, we are not denying that these sort of loving relationships do exist successfully and bring some people great happiness. But there is no truth in the idea that we can only be truly connected to one person at a time or that there aren't many equally important forms of closeness which do not involve sex.

Friendship, in the end, is often the most enduring relationship of all but that is a fact which seems to be an uncomfortable truth for capitalism.

How Does Isolation Benefit Capitalism?

A key thing that capitalism fears is the unity of the people it exploits because, if ever those people get together with a clear plan to end the exploitative relationship that exists between the capitalists and themselves, then capitalism will simply be brushed aside and a new form of society will be established. Keeping people separated from each other as much as possible is tremendously important for capitalists as they try to prolong the life of an economic system that apparently works in their favour. Persuading us that we can only love or care about a very small number of people, mostly our own relatives, is useful – possibly essential – to the maintaining of a divided and powerless society.

Virtual Relationships

A particular and relatively new threat to our ability to make real connections with each other is the ease with which we can get in touch on-line – to have 'virtual relationships' which can avoid much of the messy emotional business of a real life relationship.

In Japan, for example, a survey by the Ministry of Health, Labour and Welfare in 2010 found 36% of Japanese males aged sixteen to nineteen had no interest in sex – a figure that had doubled in the space of two years. They had taken on a mole-like existence and, worryingly, withdrawn from relationships with the opposite sex.

In a BBC News report on Oct 24th 2013, two young men, who believed themselves to be in relationships with virtual girlfriends, discussed their relationships with 'Rinko' and 'Ne-Ne'. These 'girlfriends' were actually a Nintendo computer game called Love Plus, which came as a small portable tablet.

Nurikan and Yuge described how they took their 'girlfriends', Rinko and Ne-ne, on virtual dates to the park and bought them cakes to celebrate their birthdays: "It's the kind of relationship we wish we'd had at high school" said Nurikan. In the game he was a 15-year-old, though in reality he was thirty-eight.

Yuge said he often puts Ne-ne – or the games console containing her – into the basket of his bicycle, then he took photographs of them at his destination.

"As she's at high school, she picks me up in the morning and we go to school together. After school we meet at the gates and go home together..."

Though Yuge would like to meet a real woman and Nurikan is married, they said this is easier than having a real girlfriend. "At high school you can have relationships without having to think about marriage" said Yuge, "With real girlfriends you have to consider marriage. So I think twice about going out with a 3D woman."

A comment on the website www.siliconvalleywatcher.com suggests a reason for this phenomenon:

> *"People here (in Japan) work 10 hour days, 6 days a week, for an average job. They also generally spend a couple of hours a day commuting. A part-time job is usually 5 days a week! This lifestyle starts from primary school. Kids go to school from 8–5 (or 6), and usually go to school on Saturdays for club activities, which sometimes happen Sundays as well.*

> *People have nearly no time to themselves, and I think this is the main reason that relationships suffer. People barely have time to manage their own affairs, and its when you see the average Japanese person's life in this light that you understand why relationships are 'mendokusai'. They simply don't have time. And THIS is the real problem with Japan, for Japanese people (through the eyes of an outsider); they have no relaxation time. Everything is managed to the second; everything is wound so tight. Even holidays; the average holiday is a few days, maybe once a year. There are no evenings off, no weekends off even, there is never any time to sit back, or be indulgent. Its not surprising then that sex and commitment takes a back seat to blowing off a little steam and trying to just have some fun"*

This retreat of young men into a fantasy world is one of the reasons Japan is on course for a fall of one third of its population by the year 2060. Of course it goes without saying that manufacturers of computers are reaping massive rewards from this turn of events.

CONNECTION

> *"Is there an emptiness in you as you walk your land, uneasy feet on uneasy streets, uneasy in the bedroom, uneasy even in the mirror, an uneasy creep into uneasy sleep, pulling the bedclothes up close, checking your phone, checking your phone, checking you are not here all alone, to die alone?"* **Russell Brand, 'Revolution'**

Re-connection is the only way to heal this particular hurt.

TOUCH, OUR FIRST LANGUAGE

For many of us words are not enough to close the gap between us and other people. Like a newborn baby, we need the physical touch of another human to feel safe, connected and cared for. The unfortunate narrowing of the language of touch to one which, for adults, is so often overlaid with notions of sex and sexuality, has led to most of us being deprived of one of our greatest human needs. A hug, a caress, a held hand, can all break our isolation in a moment.

Alan recalled a childhood memory which illustrates just how important a teacher's kindness was to him:

Alan "*I was about six or seven and the class teacher asked us to go and get a crate of those little milk bottles for the class. Me and my mate were running through the school – he was ahead of me and we had to go through some big double doors to the school hall and he ran through and of course the door swung back and smacked me in the eye. My eye was bleeding and it split my eyebrow and so my memory is (cries) of Miss Marsden sitting me on her lap and giving me a hug to console me I suppose. I don't remember anything else about it except her sitting me on her lap because I had been hurt.*"

Micheline: "*Why do you think you have remembered it for so long?*"

Alan: "*I don't know (cries). I guess it was what I needed at the time. Years later I discovered that she lived somewhere near to my girlfriend and I would drive past this house and think about knocking on her door and thanking her or something. It seemed really important, like it was a name I wouldn't forget. I don't remember anything about her as a class teacher or what she taught us, but I remembered this*".

Micheline: "*Why does the memory bring tears to this day do you think?*"

Alan: "*It seemed like a kindness that was really significant. I don't know how else to describe it*".

Micheline: "*If you had knocked on her door what would you have said?*"

Alan: (Cries). "*I guess I would have told her how important it was that she did that. It seems like an obvious, natural thing to do around kids, I have done it myself, but clearly – I have heard lots of talk around schools nowadays that you musn't do this sort of thing – a lot of fear about it from the adults, not the kids of course*".

Chrissie remembered with nostalgia being a teacher before such fears were dominant:

Chrissie: *"At the end of the '60s I got a job in a little village junior school way out in the countryside. I had been teaching English to 12 –15 year olds in a suburban secondary school at the time and it had been a while since I'd worked in a primary school so it came as bit of a culture shock to find myself taking 'Singing Together' with these tender little 5 and 6 year olds after tussling over 'Lord of the Flies' with moody, argumentative 15 year old boys.*

"But they all stirred my heart. The teenagers try to hide their feelings of pride or pleasure when I praised them but their body language gave them away every time. The little ones were so completely open about enjoying their relationship with you, and in those days it wasn't frowned upon to be tactile with the children. I found that holding the shy, diffident infants when they were up at my desk reading to me seemed to give them confidence - but the whole class loved a hug.

"One day when they were lining up in the classroom getting ready to go to lunch I asked if anyone wanted a hug. Down the line every hand went up but it took ages to get them to the dining room because instead of going out of the door to their dinner they'd run round to the back of the queue for 'extras'."

Free Hugs

In 2006 a social experiment was tried in New York started by one man, Juan Mann. He made placards offering free hugs and then stood on the street holding his placard to see how many people would take up the offer. So many did, some even running into his arms that the experiment turned into an international campaign of epic proportions and is still expanding. The many videos now posted on You Tube illustrate very movingly how people respond to the offer of warm physical touch even from a stranger.

The latest scientific research suggests hugging (and also laughter) is extremely effective at healing sickness, disease, loneliness, depression, anxiety and stress. According to psychologist Matt Hertenstein,

> *"It really lays the biological foundation and structure for connecting to other people".*

A good hug (more than 20 seconds) is the fastest way to get oxytocin flowing in your body. Oxytocin, also known as the "love drug", calms your nervous system and boosts positive emotions.

> *"A hug, pat on the back, and even a friendly handshake are processed by the reward centre in the central nervous system, which is why they can have a powerful impact on the human psyche, making us feel happiness and joy… And it doesn't matter if you're the toucher or touchee. The more you connect with others -- on even the smallest physical level -- the happier you'll be"*
> ***Neurologist. Shekar Raman***[4]

Like all our basic needs, capitalism will try and stop them being met naturally and freely. – 'No Touch' policies under the guise of 'child protection' in schools are one example. Not every child gets enough physical contact at home and school can offer a second chance. Bev is currently employed as a Teaching Assistant in a primary school. She spoke about how difficult she finds it to stop herself responding with physical affection to children who need it:

Bev: "I was cuddled a lot as a child, we were that sort of family. I can remember sitting in my Dad's lap when I was 35. I think that is what has allowed me to be the affectionate person I am. I work as a Teaching Assistant in a primary school so when I was told at school

---

4   Quoted in The Huffington Post

that no one was allowed to initiate a hug with any child, for fear of the 'child protection' thing, I didn't like it. In fact I cannot bring myself to not hug a child who is crying. I do it anyway because it feels so natural to me and I like to challenge the authorities on this kind of stuff. I guess I could get into trouble, but so far I haven't.

"There is a child in our school who has Down Syndrome. She is in Year 6 now so she has been in the school for several years. Her Learning Support Assistant recently told us all that no one was allowed to hug or kiss this child anymore and this really upset me. I have seen how un-engaged her parents are with her and when I was told this my eyes just filled with tears. I thought. 'Where is she going to get that love from now?'"

No Lifting Policies

Manual handling directives and their over-zealous application have also had the effect of reducing the physical contact people once received from care-givers. They have had a huge effect on disabled children and their services. Originally born out of some worrying research findings on the working days lost to the NHS because of back injuries to nurses, the reasoned response was to assess the risk to people being asked to lift heavy weights at work and to bring in measures which would minimize these risks, such as better training in lifting techniques, or the provision of mechanical support.

Somehow, however, the difference between a heavy 'load' in the factory, and a heavy human being became blurred, and blanket policies were introduced which focused on the needs of the employee without any balancing consideration of the needs of the human client who had now become a voiceless 'load'. This approach has sometimes resulted in 'no lifting' policies even for tiny children who, for example, want to be taken out of their wheelchairs and put in the sand pit with other children. Instead of a helper being trained in safe lifting techniques (and the skill of becoming 'invisible' so as not to interfere too much with a child's inclusion), mechanical mobile hoists have been introduced which need two people to operate them. So a five–year- old child trying to take part in normal play with other children suddenly finds themselves trailed around by two adults and a monster machine – hardly a recipe for 'integration'.

The extreme interpretation of these directives by some frightened adults can lead to situations which are more abusive than the 'abuse' they are trying to prevent:

Micheline: *"One memory I have emblazoned in my memory is when Lucy was in secondary school across the other side of our borough – a half-hour drive away. I got a phone call at the end of the school day from the head of 'Learning Support' to ask me to come over to the school because Lucy's wheelchair had stopped working and she couldn't move. Having asked a few questions and talked to Lucy herself on the phone, I knew that all that needed to be done was a trip switch to be pressed and the chair would spring back to life. Unfortunately this trip switch was located at the rear of Lucy's chair where she couldn't reach it herself. I told them how to do it, but they said they weren't trained and couldn't do it for health and safety reasons. I swallowed hard and said if you lift Lucy round the back of her chair (she weighed all of 3 1/2 stone), then she could do it herself. They said they couldn't do that because of their manual handling policies. I swallowed again and said, probably between gritted teeth, that her friend Suzie who was still in the school could do it as she does it all the time at our home, but of course they said that was not a possibility because of her age. Now, remember that I am myself a wheelchair user – they insisted that I got into my van and drove all the way through the traffic over to them, got out of the van into my chair, found my way around an almost deserted school with chained up doors etc, found my forlorn and deserted daughter who had been left to sit alone in the corridor to await my arrival, leaned out of my chair to lift up the lid of the compartment to press the specially designed and virtually fool-proof switch to get Lucy moving again. And 'Oh' they said, 'You had better drive her home now because her transport had been dismissed'."*

Once the natural responses of people to meet each others needs have been outlawed, it is then easy for profiteers to attempt to meet our needs through the creation of a service which has to be paid for.

Physical touch can be bought in many ways from professional massage to osteopathy. Going to the hairdressers can bring that little bit of human touch into a person's life. There are now even professional cuddlers such as 'Cuddle Up To Me' or 'The Snuggle Buddies' offering their arms to the needy for an hourly fee.

As we benefit just as much from giving hugs as we do receiving them, deciding to put any embarrassment or 'coolness' aside in order to meet this real, mutual need is a good first step in the healing process.

The Intentional Building of Community

The movement for Inclusive Education has been founded on the realisation that if disabled children grow up in isolated communities of only similarly disabled children, however kind the teachers or technically resourced their schools, their ability to connect and make friends with non-disabled children is prevented from developing and vice-versa. Consequently, children in both settings learn to see the different worlds in which they grow up as 'normal', and then these worlds become the blue-print for the adult worlds they go on to create – worlds of parallel existence even though they may be living in the same street.

Inclusive education, by contrast, sees friendship as an educational goal. This is leading to relationships between children which are barely understood by adults, but nonetheless recognised by them as profoundly important:

> *Davigdor Infants School is the main placement for William, a child with cerebral palsy who cannot speak with his own voice. Vita, Reagan, Lucy and Natasha are William's particular friends. Vita said that Natasha is usually the leader and helps him most. She is the one who can interpret what he wants. She can see his eye movements. Natasha's Mum says, "William has been fantastic for Natasha. She began by being frightened of him but now he is one of her closest friends... Natasha is more sparkly when she knows William will be in school. She gets up and says 'It's a William day today'. She never wants to miss school when he is there, even when she is ill. They have a special friendship".[5]*

The generation of young adults who have emerged from these inclusive schools are leading the sort of lives which were seen as an impossible dream for those of us who grew up in the past.

However, simply bringing people who have been historically set apart into a common space is not enough. In fact, people who currently live, work or study together can still feel isolated. To make a real connection we have to engage at a personal level.

LISTENING AS A HUMAN BRIDGE

Although our culture does not teach us the true value of listening, it is one of the most simple and effective ways of bridging the emotional gap between us. One useful way to do this is by deciding to listen to someone else whole-heartedly and without interrupting them for as many minutes as you can manage. This includes people you live with such as your family. 'Whole-heartedly' includes doing it whilst sober, switching off your mobile phone and not hoping for sex with the person you're listening to at the end of it.

---

5   From 'Snapshots of Possibility', The Alliance for Inclusive Education

You could ask them a question to start them off or you could just notice that they are needing to tell someone something but no one is listening. Giving someone your undivided attention is like building a safe corridor from their mind to yours. It is the only way to demonstrate that they are not really alone. If they feel safe enough to show emotion whilst talking to you, that is an added bonus. That is a visible sign that the corridor is open and the natural healing process is operating.

Equally effective, in terms of making a connection, is asking someone to listen to you in the same way. Tell them what you really think and try not to hide what you really feel. Think of it as a gift to them – which it is. It is a gift of authenticity. This also helps both parties to notice that they are not alone.

If both of you are comfortable with it, some physical contact, such as holding hands whilst sharing such attention can strengthen the sense of connection enormously. For most of us, as infants, touch was the first way we knew that we were not alone in the world and we need that physical reassurance still as adults.

Some people decide to formalise these times of sharing attention into 'Listening Partnerships' in which agreements are made to share equal amounts of time and other guidelines.

It is great to do this with people already in your life, especially those who may find it harder to find respectful listeners, such as children and older people. To broaden out your own picture of the world and to help further to break down the barriers between people, it is even more interesting to listen to people who are not already in your familiar circles – people from different countries, different social classes, different ethnic identities, different faiths (or no faith), different abilities or from oppressed groups you have never met.

Most challenging of all is listening to people you do not agree with or who come from opposing political views, not with a goal of arguing with them or proving them wrong but of trying to find a human commonality which can be a link between you both – something to build upon.

From Competition to Collaboration

"That's a great idea you had there Micheline, to write something about competition …… I just wish I'd had it first!" **Alan**

Our first workshop looked at universal isolation and disconnection from each other. Competition compounds this by pitting us against each other, often starting with our own brothers and sisters:

Micheline: *"I thought about my sister. She is three years older than me but for some reason or other, and I am not sure quite why, I was always told that I was the clever one. Which meant that therefore she was the 'not clever' one and we were constantly compared to one another all the time, you know, what I could do, what she could do, and I remember hating it."*

Will: *"And then there was my brother and that is the flip side of Micheline's story. He was the clever one. He passed the 11-plus and I didn't. He was very booky and into chess and that and I was into my fantasy world and that was alright. He would be the clever one and I would trundle along, pretending to be an airplane, but things didn't work out like that. I became interested in different things and he did too. I did better at school and went to university and became very interested in lots of things. He didn't have that vigorous academic experience. Now I think all that has poisoned, well altered, our relationship in ways I don't enjoy. We use language in competitive ways and we now use humour to win. If I make him laugh I think I've got something over him. I've done well."*

Competition impacts on our lives in different ways depending on where we come in the pecking order of life. In a competitive system there has to be winners and losers. If you are pre-set to be in the winning team – i.e. born into privilege and wealth – you are more likely to think of competition as a good thing than if you are born into the layers of society in which winning is unlikely. From there you will experience competition very differently. Those who more often come out on top are more likely to try and justify competition as natural and healthy than those predestined to fail.

Competition within the family is reinforced and developed by the education system as we often discover on our first day at school. Not only are we tested and ranked within school, so we can know exactly who is better than who, this competition is followed (e.g. in the UK) by: pitting school against school through publishing schools' test results in National League Tables; through comparing comprehensive education with private education and through the fierce competition to get into the university that 'really counts'.

The exam system is designed to pass or fail young people, with the results marking out a whole pre-planned future complete with types of employment possible, likely levels of pay, degrees of respect and status which can be expected and even how much influence you will find it possible to have on your world. There will be exceptions of course – people who become rich and famous having been told they were useless but in general these predictions are largely accurate. In some places in the UK, where grammar schools still exist, this sorting of the 'wheat' from the 'chaff' still occurs at just eleven years old.

Awards, medals, prizes, qualifications and titles are used to bribe us into participating in this system but by far the most effective of these is the lure of status – of 'being somebody'. This is very hard to resist because it feels like the respect we have all longed for since childhood but rarely received. Having achieved a level of status, it is harder to lose than money or things - ask anyone who has been made redundant or become disabled or simply retired from a respected career. Loss of status can lead to severe depression and even suicide.

Competition is Forced Upon Us

We do not need competition to motivate us. Most striving is about bettering our own performance, skills, mastery, learning or effectiveness because it brings us satisfaction and confidence. We are driven to develop – to 'flower' just like a living plant. By the time we are two or three years old, most of us have taught ourselves, through a process of trial and improvement, to talk and walk – two of the most difficult and complex skills we will ever have to accomplish. Most children go on to practice and succeed at: running and jumping; hanging upside down on things; riding scooters and bikes; singing and dancing; ball skills; skipping; tree climbing; drawing and painting and a multitude of other things including achieving computer skills way beyond most adults' without going near a school or a teacher.

In fact we are so energetic and enthusiastic about exploration and experimentation that most adults around us spend far more time thwarting our attempts by telling us not to do things: "Don't touch!"; "Take that out of your mouth!"; "Put it down, it's not a toy!", "Sit still!", "Be quiet!", "Do you want a smack?" and sometimes we are stopped in our tracks by simply being picked up and plonked down somewhere else. By the age of two or three we are usually able to move pretty fast and get into everything so the thwarting has to be faster and more often. If you watch this process you can see very easily that children do not like being thwarted. We all protest, often with screams and tears and do not necessarily give up without a fight. So, it is not surprising to us that this age is called the 'terrible twos' referring to the number of tantrums children seem to have. What is surprising is how most people do not seem to understand why we have them. There does not seem to be a recognition of this inner drive we all have to 'become ourselves' or how painful it is to not be able to fulfill it even though the evidence is all around and within us.

Collaboration Makes Life Work

Without our ability to collaborate the human race would be stuffed.

The food we eat, the clothes we wear, the houses we live in are all produced by vast numbers of people working together including farmers, transport workers, fashion designers, sewing machine operators, brick makers, architects, builders and thousands of others.

Alan: "When I was young I worked in factories and especially around here where there were car factories, and despite the competition between firms, there was no way they could survive without a very well organised collaborative effort to make sure things were made on time, delivered on time, arrived at the assembly track on time – things being put together in the right order. This is how people have made progress."

Our services, upon which we rely to: move us about; educate our children; treat us when we are ill; care for us when we are unable; arrive at our burning houses in a matter of minutes because we pressed the number nine three times on our phones and so on, are all testaments to our amazing capacity to build co-operative teams of people working for the common good.

The worldwide work of charities and not-for-profit campaigns and pressure groups achieve life-saving feats everyday, ranging from the rescuing of the little Spoon-Billed Sandpiper from the brink of extinction, to rapidly bringing food and medicine to victims of natural disasters or wars.

As individuals, we can achieve very little. We could not survive our first few days of life if no one came to feed us, hold us, wrap us up and love us. We are not designed for a solitary life. Collaboration is natural to us.

Capitalism, however, brings its own, different value system which it then imposes upon us.

Alan: "*We can't imagine how the National Health Service in the UK would work without the co-operation of everybody – the cleaners, nurses, doctors, specialists, administrators - it is a massive co-operative effort. Building a house: painters, decorators, bricklayers, plumbers all need to come together to make it work. So, in a way, we are very used to it on one level but the light is not shone on collaboration in the same way that you hear people constantly promoting the importance of competition*".

Capitalism is the latest of a long line of triangular shaped systems invented by humans to benefit the small number of people who live at the top point of the pyramid, at the cost of the majority of people at the bottom of the pyramid. All triangular systems, now and in the past, have people in the middle, bribed in one way or another, to manage the whole thing, be they standing armies, barons, knights, professionals or bureaucrats but they are still beholden to the people at the top.

THE MYTH OF SCARCITY

For this triangular system to work we all need to be convinced that it is somehow natural and normal, that we all deserve our designated places because there isn't enough in the world for all of us. "We can't all be winners can we?"

From our earliest childhood we are steeped in the notion that life is a competition and the best thing we can do is: try to win; to do better than others and to strive to come top. To do otherwise is to fail and to be poor, weak, disrespected, excluded and who would want that?

Even if we are lucky enough to have parents who do not subscribe to this notion, who encourage: sharing; kindness and equality amongst themselves and their children, the minute we are compelled to go to school, sometimes as young as three, we soon learn that the name of the game is competition, competition, competition. The whole system is designed to fill the triangle, preparing our innocent children for their life ahead.

Tim B: *"My early experiences with competition were very much out at school competing with other children because I was raised an insecure little boy and had an 'inferiority complex' as it was called at the time. I needed to be in a group of other people who would find other kids to look down on so that is where the competition really came from. To be able to be superior in some way to at least one other little boy to make sure I could feel good about myself".*

Our parents' current place in the triangle will mostly determine the expected outcome of school regardless of the individual child's abilities or passions. Only a small number of 'exceptional' children break free of this and most of *them* seem to live in perpetual fear that they will be found out to be imposters, pretending to be cleverer than they really are.

The world of work is the 'reality' for which we were all being groomed. All work in the capitalist system is aimed at one thing – making a profit. If the enterprise doesn't do that, it dies along with its owners, workers and customers. It is as simple as that. Winning the competition for customers is what makes it work and everyone, including the 'owners' have absolutely no choice about playing this game:

Dania: *"My father was a business man but, unfortunately for us, a very bad one so he went through many cycles and crises. He was intensely competitive and when the business was up it was fine but when the business went down it was our family that paid the cost of his competitiveness. My mother is a South African who had moved to India and I remember times when she went to shop for these very* *nice clothes like she had in South Africa. I also remember, as a child, times when she had to display these clothes on the furniture and the neighbours would come and buy the clothes because there was no money in the house"*

To stay in the game you have to be better than the others. Your products have to be cheaper or of a higher quality or more original or innovative. Your workforce has to be more skilled, hard-working, compliant, reliable, less demanding and cheaper than others in the field. Your raw materials have to be sourced at the cheapest rates and your transport and overhead costs have to be the lowest.

As a potential employee, this means you have to get used to the idea of beating the other applicants for every job you might want. You have to have the best qualifications, the slickest CV, the most glowing references, a good track record of extra-curricular activities, look nice, dress well, have a pleasant manner, speak good English, exude relaxed confidence, be not too fat, hairy or smelly, be decidedly not pregnant or planning to be, never ill, no sign of disability, experienced but not too old and be able to talk animatedly and enthusiastically about toilet cleaning or marine biology (or whatever the job entails). You also have to be able to withstand the numerous unexplained rejections, gather up your battered ego and try again – especially when you are young and vulnerable - and that is before you have even started the job!

To help us accept all this, the habits of competitive thinking are drummed into us very early. The majority of children in the industrialised world watch the television from infancy onwards and are subjected to thousands of advertisements well before they enter the education system. We start off believing them.

Micheline*: "I remember my daughter at the age of about four, lecturing me about floor cleaners, a subject about which she felt she had some expertise, as she had just watched something about a 'White Tornedo' whilst waiting for Sesame Street to start. She treated my* *explanation about the falseness of the advertisement messages with great cynicism. After all, she had seen it with her own eyes!"*

This conditioning continues when, as children, we are constantly tested and examined, with scores ranked against our class mates for all to see. It happens when our best friend is siphoned off into the 'Gifted and Talented' programme at school and we are left behind in the ungifted and talentless sub-class of 'losers'. It happens when our sister passes her entrance exam to a fancy school and we don't or when we get picked for the football team and our friend with asthma has to sit and resentfully watch us being part of the fun.

University seems to be the final gateway of no return. Once there, you become one of the 'superior' ones, whatever your original status in life. You will always be thought of as being 'better than' those who didn't make it, whatever you think yourself. Conversely, those who do not go to university often think of themselves as intellectually inferior – more suited to the sort of work that doesn't seem to require so much thinking.

It is not easy to squash our natural desire to work in mutual co-operation and to replace it with a desire to beat our friends or sisters and brothers at everything, especially as they often hate you for it. Adults have to do all sorts of things to force youngsters to conform. The adults themselves have to have had the same or similar treatment when they were young in order to be convinced it is the only way and that they are in fact doing their child a service, protecting them from the hard life ahead if they don't succeed.

The competitive message is strong but not natural to us therefore we need it reinforced every day of our lives if possible so we keep believing it. Unfortunately that has become very easy.

Every day most of us spend far too much time slumped in front of the television. The broadcasting companies that bring us our entertainment are either profit-driven enterprises in their own right, depending for their survival on income from advertisements, or

the so-called 'public service' British Broadcasting Corporation (the BBC) which depends on the approval of the government of the day who ultimately have control. This foundation does not lend itself to piercing critiques of the effects of capitalism; reporting on inspiring examples of alternative economic systems or showing significant stories of successful grass-roots actions around the world. Mostly it lends itself to trying to convince us that life, as we know it, is perfectly normal, fair and 'the only way'.

Competition is the theme of so many light entertainment programmes that you could be forgiven for thinking it is a deliberate plan to make us unthinkingly accept the growing inequality all around us – the 1% winners versus the 99% losers.

This form of 'entertainment' stepped up in popularity, in the UK, in the year 2000 with the advent of the *'Big Brother'* house. An experimental TV programme on Channel 4 corralled a number of young adults, handpicked for their differences, into a house for a number of weeks where they were watched by millions of viewers as they talked, cried, fought, negotiated and lied their way to be the last one remaining after their housemates and the viewers voted each week to evict people from the fold. The winner got a valuable monetary prize plus enormous publicity. The others got nothing except varying degrees of notoriety and humiliation. The public loved it. They happily took an active part in the outcome of the show by telephoning in their vote as to who should stay and who should go. Power at last.

Buoyed by this success, variations on this apparently hugely popular formula for a television show has now been imposed on a breathtaking range of subjects from holding dinner parties to singing in a choir. It has been applied to cooking, sewing, interior design, and even (May 2014) growing things on allotments! Every pleasant, creative and collaborative activity that we choose to relax and enjoy ourselves, free from the judgement of others, has been packaged into a competitive nightmare where all the contestants have to strive to be better than each other in order to avoid public failure and exclusion.

'*The Apprentice*', a programme in which a small number of hopefuls compete for a six-figure salaried job with Sir Alan Sugar, probably takes this to its most ruthless extreme. Fellow contestants fall over themselves to justify to 'Sir' why the person sitting by them is an incompetent waste-of-space and should be fired whilst they themselves are just shit-hot stuff and should be hired.

Talent shows such as '*The X Factor*' and '*Strictly Come Dancing*' follow the same basic formula of competition and elimination. In all these programs there are significant prizes and titles to be won. There can only ever be *one* winner.

There is an excitement in watching this. An adrenaline rush is carefully manufactured by the program makers as we hold our breaths, hearts racing, for those few silent moments of tension after the words "… and the person to leave is …." as we hear the name of the poor unfortunate who is to be sent packing. We watch in a mixture of wordless pain and confusion as the hurts of this are felt and shown by the contestants – the falling faces, the attempts to cover up the disappointment, the tears, the goodbye hugs, the resigned goodbye speech, the sly head-to-camera films of the current survivors saying how much so-and-so will be missed - relief pouring off them like steam from a kettle. We, the watchers, are supposed to rejoice in the happiness of the winner and just accept the pain we have all been forced to witness as somehow 'worth it'. But in our hearts we don't.

The hopeful part of this is that, despite the relentless attempts to pit us against each other, we still resonate with empathy when a fellow human suffers defeat. Even when we are the winner, we can never really fully rejoice in our achievements when we feel it to be at someone else's cost. Life under this system is deeply confusing.

To add to the confusion, at the same time as being encouraged to compete and win, we are *simultaneously* being encouraged to be 'team members': to not put each other down; to encourage each other to succeed and to remember we are just little cogs in a great big wheel. Diversity is increasingly valued and 'Different but Equal' is a mantra in many schools striving to be inclusive. This is because of the underlying contradiction between our inherent human needs and the needs of the system.

Dania: "Capitalism is all about markets. You have to change the way people think in order to sustain markets. Social relationships are changed from friendship and co-operation to competitive – it is almost like a moral framing. Relationships are reconstructed and that is how capitalism survives."

There *are* enough resources in the world to go round if we all took our 'fair share'. At some level we all know this and that we only survive because we can work together for goals outside of ourselves. But, even though we know this, even when the compulsion from outside stops, because, for example, we have left education or paid employment, we are driven by the inner compulsions caused by our accumulated hurts to continue to think, feel and sometimes act, competitively.

Jennifer: "I think there is somewhere within us where it is natural that we should come together and work for the benefit, not just for ourselves, but for each other and that we do it and there are examples of it all over society and the competitiveness is what comes in and disrupts that and causes friction. So you might have a group that works well together but, at some point, some element from outside or from within, breaks it up by putting the element of competition within it."

Micheline: "Back in my twenties I belonged to this thing called 'The Alternative Society' which was a very radical thing at the time. We went on a 'holiday' and, I put inverted commas around the word, it was a gathering of families and other people. The heading was a 'Craft Camp' and I went as a craft teacher but the real idea was to get people together to create a community. We turned up in a disused farmhouse that had no lights working, no cooker, no tables, no chairs, no flushing toilets, very young children and 30 people who didn't know each other. Somebody vaguely took charge and found out all the skills of the people who were there – 'What do you do? What do you bring? We need a stove. Can anybody wire it in?' Within three hours a second-hand stove had been found and collected, wired in, tables had been made from old doors found outside, oil drums had been found to balance them on, benches made, beds made upstairs, septic tank had been cleared out and the toilets were flushing. I have never forgotten this experience. We all had something to do - even me. I thought, 'Well, you could do that with any group of people at any time'."

A dog-eat-dog world ends up with one dog with nothing to eat. We survive because we collaborate at every step of the way but this self-evident truth is barely acknowledged because to do so might allow us to 'revert' to our real natures and perhaps notice that no one really wants to eat dogs.

From Addiction to Rationality

The most lethal consumer product in the world is a cigarette. The six trillion cigarettes that are sold every year worldwide owe their attraction to the sole fact that nicotine is an addictive drug. The selling of this product kills five million of its buyers every year. The success of the industry can be measured in the numbers of deaths it causes.

Although the industry itself claims that they only target adults, who are given all the information they need to make a 'free choice' about whether to smoke or not, most new smokers are children. In the UK 200,000 young people aged eleven to fifteen start smoking every year. The industry needs them in order to replace the smokers they are losing to lung disease, cancer and related health problems later in life.

Despite the health warnings, now out in the open, the industry worldwide makes £30 million pounds in profits every year and that figure is steadily growing. In the UK our exchequer also benefits because income from taxes on the sale of cigarettes still amounts to twice the cost to the NHS of treating patients with smoking related diseases. In terms of capitalist economics, smoking is a resounding success.

Alcohol is perhaps the second most dangerous legalised addictive substance sold in our shops, pubs, clubs and restaurants. One short extract from the 'Coventry Telegraph' (June 6th 2014) under the front page headline 'CITY'S ALCOHOL ABUSE SHAME' hints at the scale of the problem:

"Drinkers are admitted to hospital in Coventry and Warwickshire at a rate of one every 30 minutes.... Local NHS staff had to deal with 17,420 hospital admissions in just a year just because of alcohol abuse"... Dr. Jas Grewal, a Coventry consultant psychiatrist specialising in alcohol addiction says, "It is a national problem with one in three adults misusing alcohol".

These are just two examples of the countless ways profit is made from our human vulnerability rather than our human needs.

It seems that we humans can become addicted to almost anything. It is not just cigarettes or the well-understood nightmare of being hooked on heroin or cocaine or being an alcoholic but the hundreds of different ways we are pulled to do the same thing over and over again, even when we know it is bad for us, like eating bars of chocolate or watching porn on our computers, or gambling away our only income or watching boring soaps on the telly or being fascinated by women's breasts or hoarding old newspapers until there is no room to sit down or buying shoes you may never wear or falling in love with unsuitable people ..... the list goes on. The problem is not necessarily the act itself, you could be addicted to 'good' things, helping other people for example or cleaning your house – it is the *compulsion to do it repeatedly* that hi-jacks our lives.

Not everyone who has a drink becomes an alcoholic and not everyone who eats a biscuit cannot stop until the packet is empty. Why do some people seem more vulnerable to addictive behaviours than others? Clearly the reasons are complex and include our sensitivity to chemicals in food, drink and drugs, both legal and illegal, but something else is going on too.

Frozen Needs

When a real human need is not met, particularly in a child, that is a 'hurt' and it becomes embedded in our minds along with all the feelings that went with it – longing, loneliness, anxiety, hunger and so on. These feelings drive us to try and fill the need forever more. For example, the need for closeness and community in our societies is often unfilled in children and this can leave us desperately *wanting to be wanted* by our peer group – to feel we belong. In one study, the main reason young people gave when asked about why they started smoking was:

> *"All my friends smoked and I didn't want to be left out"*
> **'Burning Desire – The Seduction of Smoking' - BBC2**
> **programme June 2014**

This need far outweighed the effects of the graphic health warnings on the packets or the significant dent in their small incomes, to which they barely gave a second thought – "With all the smokers in the world why should it be me that gets ill?"

But when we try to fill an unmet childhood need as an adult, something strange happens. Whatever you find to fill that need never seems quite enough. Even if at first you think, 'Ah this is it, heaven! I am now satisfied'. After a while it turns out to be not quite as good as you thought – the shoes don't quite fit or the partner doesn't love you enough or 'just one doughnut' doesn't quite do the trick. The need has become 'frozen' and un-fillable. These hurts result in repetitive and futile attempts to fill the frozen needs. These hurts can attach themselves to almost anything, especially things that remind us in some way of the early need and they can manifest themselves as addictions.

Russell Brand, infamous for his addictions to sex and drugs, spoke eloquently about this phenomena when giving evidence to a governmental select committee on drug addiction in 2012:

> *"The reason I took drugs was because of emotional and psychological difficulties – a spiritual malady perhaps. I was sad, lonely, unhappy and detached. Drugs and alcohol seemed the solution. It was only when I tried the abstinence-based approach to recovery and dealt with these issues that I didn't need the drugs anymore."*

Drug addiction is not only about the drugs we buy out of 'choice'. We in the developed world are heavily addicted to prescribed drugs, including drugs to stop us feeling our own pain. For example, in 2014 it was reported that 10% of the entire population of the UK take anti-depressants. (See Mental Health System Oppression on page 111.)

The part of our human make-up that is vulnerable to addiction is very useful to a system which wants us to buy stuff we don't really need.

I remember when I was at art college being in a lecture about the psychology of graphic design in advertisements and how it is used to manipulate people's emotions. The design of OMO soap powder for example, was based on the face of an owl with two big eyes and a downward pointing 'beak' in the middle. This particular configuration in nature arrests our attention so it helped draw the eye of a potential consumer to that particular brand of soap powder competing with others on a supermarket shelf. I remember also learning that the colour blue is associated in our minds with a sweet taste and so is often used to sell bags of sugar.

The most successful advertisements are the ones that recognise these needs within us and persuade us that buying their product will somehow fill that need. Remember BT's 'It's good to talk' advertisements? Signing up to a contract with the phone company was going to lead to long intimate chats with your friends even when you didn't know what to say to them when you actually met them.

A 'frozen need' is a real human need which should have been met when we were children but was left unmet. For example the need for affection. Leaving such a need unmet is a hurt, and these hurts result in rigid feelings of need even when we become adults – but 'frozen' needs can never be filled.

A Never Ending Market

In terms of selling us stuff, it is a great advantage to producers that we have these sort of 'needs' because they lead us to feel we can never get enough of anything to stop us wanting more. As most of our real, emotional needs, past and present, can only really be filled by close relationships with other people and these are, by definition, 'free of charge', the wheels of commerce are made to spin by attempting to break our direct relationships with other people and then selling us something which promises to re-connect us again. Manufacturing new addictions, manipulating our 'frozen needs' and then selling us the 'fix' we then crave are two of the most damaging aspects of capitalism. We never feel we have enough, so we keep on buying.

There were recently two series of documentaries on the television (Jacques Peretti, BBC 2, August 2013). Series One was called '*The Men Who Made Us Fat*'. It began by telling the story of the replacement of sugar by corn syrup in the manufacture of processed foods in the USA in the 1970's – a time when farming was being developed on an industrial scale. This syrup is made from the deliberately created surplus of corn produced by cattle-feed farmers. The syrup was sweeter than sugar and a third cheaper. The sweeter the food, the more people bought. It was addictive. When, in 1984, the soft drink industries replaced sugar with corn syrup these drinks became the biggest source of calories in the USA. As a result the average weight of all USers has risen by three stone.

Here in Britain, the food industry, which does not have access to surplus corn, instead created a culture of snacking on sweet, sugary, fatty foods (remember 'A Mars a day helps you work, rest and play'?). Exacerbated by the import of fast-food and soft drinks from the USA, we Brits are now, on average, also three stone heavier than we were 50 years ago. Two-thirds of Brits are overweight and one in four is obese – a state which is classified as a disease.

The second series was called '*The Men Who Made Us Thin*'. Here Jacques Peretti told the story of how the harm that had been inflicted on people by the first group of men had created new and lucrative markets for another set of profit-seekers in the form of diet books, programmes, diet foods, exercise machines, gyms, fitness trainers and so on. Just think about all the new clothes we have to buy as our body shape balloons and shrinks constantly like the tide going in and out.

This relationship between the creation of addictions, by markets which profit from them, is applicable to all the forms taken by our addictions. It is hard to think of an addiction that is not lining someone's pocket with gold.

Industries that feed people's addictions may provide the means to earn a living for some people but they can in no way be seen as providing meaningful work. To engage in these industries requires a suspension of our morality – our conscience. We learn the art of self-delusion and justification in order to carry on churning out the product but we are wounded by this. This is a hurt.

Feeding addictions also requires massive resources such as land and water that should be used to answer real needs such as nutrition. Addictions also waste our time and effort far more than we like to think or admit.

The damage is not only from our own addictions but the effect of other people's addictions – especially our loved ones – on our lives, which can of course be devastating.

Towards Rationality

There are only two certain ways of healing these hurts and neither is easy.

The vulnerability to addictions will always be present in human beings but without the profit motive to stoke it up into gigantic proportions, we could build societies that help to protect us from this possibility.

The best way is to create a world that answers our basic human needs right from the start. This could be much more simple and possible than it sounds because we already know what our needs are and how to meet them. It is much cheaper than any other way and won't destroy the Earth in its wake. The problem is how to *stop* doing all the other stuff.

Once addiction has set in, the only other way, as advocated by Russell Brand, is to stop acting on the addictive pull (i.e. give up smoking) and allow ourselves to feel the underlying unmet need. This is not to be masochistic but to give ourselves a chance to do the emotional healing that we need to do in relation to our early lives. His point was that people need *help* and not punishment for their addictions. He argued that we should stop thinking we have solved the problem of addiction by replacing an illegal drug such as heroin with a prescription drug such as methadone but to find much more funding for programmes which are founded on compassion and ongoing support to maintain a drug-free recovery. Although he stopped using drugs ten years ago, he said he still needs the support and fellowship of former addicts to stay on the right path:

> *"When I was in treatment it was explained to me that I couldn't use drugs or drink, one day at a time. This was an anathema to me: my life, identity and ability to cope on the most fundamental level were all dependent on substance use. I could not countenance even the most trivial interactions without some kind of chemical wetsuit to protect me. When I was introduced to the concept of 'getting to bed that night without using' I was afraid and suspicious. The fear had become a prison whose walls I could not breach.*
> *"Without the compassion of others, the support and encouragement of people who had been through what I was going through, and learned to live a different life, I would never have been able to stop. Through them I saw a vision of how I could live differently. If people whose problems had been more serious than mine could stop, then perhaps I could. More important than that, the feelings they described were the same as the ones I was experiencing. This gave me something life had lacked until that point: community. Common unity."* **Russell Brand, 'Revolution'**

It is very hard for us to overcome major addictions on our own and it can be hard to find people with the time to listen and the level of skills and sensitivity needed in order to make it safe for us to reach the buried feelings and to allow ourselves to talk, laugh, rage, shake or cry them off our shoulders for ever.

Lucy speaks about the struggle that many young people face when looking for help (attention) to deal with the confusion caused by a youth culture which seems to require the use of addictive substances or to run the risk social exclusion:

Lucy: "If you feel judged, it's just going to exacerbate it (the addictions) 'cos it always comes from a place of feeling shit in the first place, so it just doesn't help... I think there's got to be some flexibility around it because clearly a lot of people who have done amazing things and have thought amazing things and have led social movements have been people with addictions. It's not a complete nulling and voiding of your brain."

Micheline: "I think the thing about addictions for me is, of course the people who've got them are not to blame, but I think what I can sort of see in my mind's eye is a cosmic capitalist, raking in the money by peddling these things which do two things: keep people, you know, sedated for want of a better word and not fighting back and also creating masses of money for themselves – masses of money. So, they're laughing their heads off and it's that I can't bear!"

Lucy: "The point though, it's like, that's TRUE, that it is part of the capitalist system but it's no more a part than a lot of other quite horrible things about capitalism but it's one of the things where people have no space (to listen). It's like, "NO!". There's no space around it and I think it just doesn't help people to be very honest about their difficulties".

Micheline: "I can understand that."

Lucy: "People will be less addicted if they're building closer relationships. I think you've got to start by letting people build the closer relationships and then it will happen quite organically rather than like diving at it. If you're talking about helping young people organize and stuff."

Alan: "What addictions have you got in mind Lucy? What do you think are the big ones that your generation face?"

Lucy: "Alcohol is probably the biggest one actually although it's maybe not the one we talk about the most. It's a social addiction. I don't think that most people of my age are 'alcoholics' in the sense that they go out and drink every day but when young adults are together, probably, once there's more than three or four of you, the likelihood is that there will be alcohol. I would think if you go out, it's quite likely that you'd have alcohol. If you go out to eat a meal it's quite likely. If you go out to a party it's more than likely. I think weed is probably the next one and cigarettes …. and then, I think also, that recreational drugs are really, really prevalent as a way of people blowing off steam, (trying to) get closer to each other or feeling things they don't get to feel a lot of the time. They're addictions, but not in the same way. Like, we do it all the time but they're part of the social culture. And then others like T.V. and food and fashion and make-up and relationships, money - there's loads! We're all addicted to loads of stuff but those are the ones that are the most destructive I think."

Alan: *"And you said that you thought that was different for your generation. Could you say a bit more about that?"*

Lucy: *"I think addictions have become a lot more prevalent and I think that, if you want to get really close to young adults, you have to be around young adults that are smoking and drinking and doing those things without being disapproving of it every time – that's going to be important. It's not that we don't think this is a problem, I'm not saying that but I think that you've got to have the attention for it. That's what I mean.*

"I think you'd be shocked. I think your generation don't have a clear picture of how prevalent that stuff is 'cos we don't get to tell you. Like, I think most of my friends would lie to their parents about that stuff."

But Ben points out that it may not be as hard as we think:

"I'm trying to think about that ability to listen and to not freak out. It's not just about being non-judgemental but it's also about being able to ride with uncertainty so, you know, in times of crisis, what I'm NOT looking for in my allies is someone who can just ride in and fix anything, but to just be there with me".

From Materialism to Sustainability

> *"The great danger in today's world, pervaded as it is by consumerism, is the desolation and anguish born of a complacent yet covetous heart, the feverish pursuit of frivolous pleasures, and a blunted conscience. Whenever our interior life becomes caught up in its own interests and concerns, there is no longer room for others, no place for the poor"* **Pope Francis 2014**

In the 'developed' world the foundations of 'materialism' start early. Most of us have memories of deriving great pleasure out of a few, very special things, especially when we were young:

Ayana: "I remember I had a doll I was given for Christmas when I was four and she was like my really best friend growing up"

Things that allow us to develop our imaginations or talents are particularly important:

Micheline: "Toys! Toys at Christmas. I loved toys and we didn't have many, so getting something new to play with was a big excitement. Particularly for me, what I loved was something like a box of Meccano, something I could do something with, you know."

Alan: "I always think the things I want to hang onto are my musical instruments. The rest can go. I wouldn't like to lose those (laughs)."

The problem is when we start wanting things we don't need:

Susan: "It's like when my friend tells me about something she has bought and I think "I need one of those!" even though the idea of it was something I didn't know existed – I had no concept of this thing that cleans fucking stairs you know".

Ayana: *"It happens to me a lot where I look at something and think I don't really need that and then something happens inside my mind where I imagine if I had that object, how would it make me feel or I think where I would put it. In the end, for me, it is how I imagine it would make me feel".*

Micheline: *"There are only a few areas I can be convinced to buy things I don't actually need. Plants is one. Take me to a garden centre and I am an addict. And books, you know, there is never an end to the books I would like to buy".*

For industry to be profitable, we all have to go shopping in order to buy the products that are made. We have to continually get new stuff to wear, to plaster our faces with, to clutter up our shelves and drawers, to drive around in, to eat, smoke and drink. If we cannot be persuaded that we need much more stuff, we can be persuaded to endlessly buy experiences:

Tim K: *"What was important for my parents and it has continued for me, was having nice holidays and also going to see concerts and going to the theatre and so on. And the best too – Wimbledon Theatre was not as good as Sadler's Wells!"*

Because we have to work hard for the means to buy stuff, we have to really like shopping. We have to believe the things we can buy will make-up for the things we lose in the 'rat race' of paid employment.

In his book *'To Have Or To Be'* the social psychologist Erich Fromm warned us that we were being shaped by this system into a different kind of human being – one who felt his or her identity was defined by his or her possessions (the 'To Have' mode of existence):

"If I am what I have, and lose what I have, then who am I?"
Erich Fromm

Ayana: "For me growing up, having things was very important, to such a point that it's kind of your identity, who you are, and how you are seen as a family. I felt I was judged by what I had. When I look back now over my life, we always had enough, more than enough but growing up it always felt we needed to have more."

Fromm said that, as such, we would live with a perpetual sense of insecurity as our possessions could always be taken from us. This, he said, was not a fear of losing our stuff but of losing *ourselves.*

Tim K: "My Mum was a refugee from Nazi Germany so my experience of growing up was of being a child of a refugee. One of the things I learned from her was that the things you have got in your head, they can't take that away from you but the material things you have got, they can"

The memory of poverty can create 'frozen (unfillable) needs' around security:

Ayana: "My Dad, having come from a family with low income, he wanted a better life. I remember him telling us that as a young person he would go out at night to use the street lights because they didn't have any lighting at home and he would sit on the street and use the street light to study so he could get himself educated. And he did that, getting qualifications, so he could get better jobs and a good life. Growing up we were always reminded of his experience. He started his own business, which led to another business and that to another business. So, I grew up in a home where having things was important to secure a 'good' life but if you compared it to most people who had to work very hard every day to make ends meet, we had enough but it wasn't so - we always had to have more."

Tim K: *"We didn't have that many nice things because my Mum, who on the one hand was very generous, was also very mean. You know, she would stint on food even though she could afford to eat much more opulently, like she was saving up for a rainy day which never seemed to come".*

Such memories can lead to a constant drive to be upwardly mobile:

Alan: *"We moved out of the council estate when I was a teenager, when my parents bought their first home. After that I think they moved home eight times, I counted them last night. It seemed like a joke in the family you know, that they we constantly moving – slightly bigger, slightly better – me and my brothers we got tired you know, because we had to be there, humping the bloody furniture, helping them redecorate constantly! We used to say to my Mum, "This is the last time" but she didn't stop and they ended up living in a very nice house on the edge of Coventry, five bedrooms, double garage even after all their children had left home. Eventually the penny dropped that it was too big for them. They were getting on and they moved into this flat on the top floor of the building my mother lives in now. Of course, that wasn't good enough until suddenly one of the flats on the ground floor became available which had a conservatory and led onto the garden and which was the only property which had direct access on to the garden so of course they bought that! They moved downstairs! (laughs).*
I think, if it had been left to my Dad, probably we would still be living on the council estate."

Micheline: *"I am not really wedded to any of my stuff but what I am wedded to is having money in the bank. It really is my security. I absolutely know that below a certain point I begin to feel very, very insecure. Also, that point goes up as time goes on. In fact, it goes up with the amount of money in my bank account! (laughs)... my feeling about giving away my money is that I would be giving away my* *insurance policy against destitution and institutionalisation. Because I can't trust people… I need £6000 in my savings account or I feel really anxious. I don't know where that particular sum has come from but, you know, my daughter, she lives with a minus bank account! How can anyone sleep with a minus bank account?" (laughs).*

Advertising, peer pressure and competition are fundamental tools that capitalists use to make us constantly want more:

Susan: *"When did I start wanting things? We used to go to my cousins' and all sit round and watch the little telly. I think it was when the telly came in and you could see the things you could have - that there were different ways of living."*

Privilege and inequality hurts both sides, especially when we are young:

Ayana: *"And going to a private school, that is where the competition grew – being contaminated by seeing what other people had. I remember we noticed each other, everyone knew what you had. Although we went to an all girls' school and everyone wore uniforms, if you had new shoes or if you had something in your hair or new earrings or bracelet, everyone would know. As soon as you entered the school, we chanted; "Sssssssss" and there goes this sound… Every time you wore something new it was noticed. It was really horrid. The teachers never stopped it".*

Tim K: *"My brother and I grew up in a large house with a bedroom each. My wife had grown up in a small three-bedroom flat. Her parents slept in one room, whilst she slept in another room with her two sisters and the four brothers all slept in one room. Their flats had a shared courtyard that all the children played in. The flat did not have its own outdoor space so when she first came over to visit me at my parents' home, in the second half of the '70s, she saw our house, which she thought was a mansion, and our garden, which she thought was*

a park. It wasn't really that big, I guess it just seemed like that to her,
coming from such a small home.
"She was one of seven children and they each thought that they were
the special one. I was one of two and we each thought that we were
the disappointment. Those two 'facts' show to me that happiness does
not come from the ownership of material goods."

But the problem is not just the effect on our personal happiness. The natural resources upon which we depend to fill the shops do not get more plentiful. For example we have same amount of water on our planet, to the drop, that we had billions of years ago. Despite the fact that it changes form constantly by evaporation, condensation, freezing, melting and passing through living tissues, it still comes out as water in the end. We cannot create water. We cannot create anything from nothing. The only thing we can do through industrial processes is contaminate, pollute and transform base elements into new configurations by mixing them up into alloys, resulting in reducing their usefulness to us. Around one fifth of the world's population now suffers from a shortage of fresh water because of our industrial processes that contaminate it with chemicals.

In her book 'The Story of Stuff' Annie Leonard started a life-changing journey of discovery. She took an everyday object she owned and asked herself how it had been made. It was like drawing back a veil on an intricate scene she had only previously witnessed through a pin-hole in the curtain.

It starts with the *extraction* of raw materials, mining and harvesting. Extraction industries are not usually in towns where we can see them but far away in distant and remote areas where the working conditions of employees and the environmental degradation they cause are out of sight.

Then there is *production* in factories and workshops around the world, using huge quantities of natural resources (it takes about thirty six gallons of water to make one cup of coffee and 256 gallons to make one T-shirt) and creating many deadly poisons and harmful emissions which are poured out into the environment.

Then there is *distribution* – how stuff is moved around the planet in boats, planes, trains and trucks – all using fuel and further polluting the air we breathe and the water we drink.

Then there is *disposal*, especially of industrial waste. (Annie Leonard cited 76% of all waste in the USA as originating in the production of our stuff.) Apart from the problem of our wastefulness – throwing away a third of all the food we buy for example – we are having to find more and more land to bury our rubbish, land which then becomes unusable for anything else.

Retail, the bit we do see, is designed to make us feel good about spending our money. The prices we pay for the items we buy nowhere near cover the actual cost of their production when all these things are taken into account. If it did we couldn't afford to buy them. The system works by stealing from the common pot of natural resources and hoping no one notices or understands the long-term implications of doing so.

Increasingly though, we are becoming aware that this whole story will not have a happy ending. We have been warned by scientists and environmentalists for many decades that there are limits to growth on a finite planet. More recently, we are becoming emotionally aware of the delusion of buying our way to fulfillment.

Doing something about it is easy in some ways but requires constant mental effort. It is a form of swimming against the tide.

It is probable that we humans have already extracted all we need from the earth and could leave the rest alone, along with its carbon. We could do with less, mend things, re-use things, re-cycle things, give things away to people who need them more. We could make and grow more of our own stuff. We could make things that last. We could share more. Many of us who are older still have memories of a less materialistic age:

Susan: "My Mum and Dad made things and toys. We had a blackboard and my Dad made us a little toy house – well it was a bungalow so it could go under the bed. You know, there was all this home made stuff that was really lovely so I don't remember wanting things particularly."

Micheline: "Buying things wasn't a big thing in our family. You didn't pay other people, you made things yourself. My Mum and my Dad made everything. We bought the raw materials to make things, like cloth and patterns. My Gran knitted and my Mum made all our clothes".

Susan: "My parents weren't ambitious either. They seemed content with their lot and they loved and appreciated us. They were content with who we were too. My Dad was delighted having two little girls. Being satisfied with not much - that was a sort of class thing (low expectations) but what was wrong with it?"

Alan: "My parents were very strict about not getting into debt. It was a very principled thing you know. If you wanted to buy something you saved the money - not to get it on the 'never never' as it was called then. That was the road to ruin. They did buy a car but my mother, who was a cleaner, tells the story of how she used to clean flats and houses on our council estate prior to the new families moving in. She cleaned sixty houses at a pound a time - sixty houses for the sixty pounds to buy their first car."

SUSTAINABILITY

Alan: "In my bedroom there's a set of small drawers where I keep my socks, pants and T-shirts. At any one time I only wear ONE pair of socks, ONE pair of pants and ONE t-shirt. The rest of my things spend most of their lives sitting in one of my drawers. I had so many socks in my drawer that when I bought some new winter socks recently, I had to throw out some older socks to ensure I could open and close the drawer properly. I began to realise that most of what I own – not just clothing – I don't use most of the time.

"My car sits at the roadside an average of about twenty-three hours a day (I'm either sleeping, at work or in the house). I have: a ladder; a good selection of hand tools from small Swiss files to a large felling-axe, with all sorts of screw drivers and spanners in between; several small, hand-operated machine tools including a drill, a sander, a wood planer and a router; a trolley jack which I use if I ever need to lift my car; a chain-saw and a hedge-trimmer. Most of these things are used less than three or four times a year. My guess is that I'm not the only person in my local community who has a storage problem because they have so many clothes – many of which they hardly ever or never wear. And I imagine I'm not the only person with a reasonably good selection of tools that are used very infrequently – and who also struggles to do certain jobs for the want of the correct tools for that particular job.

"Imagine having a community tool store that was really well stocked with good quality tools that you could borrow when you needed them – much the same as we do when we borrow a book from the library. Such a resource could have every conceivable type of hand or machine tool that you might ever need when doing some maintenance or DIY work at home."

Sustainability is, in a way, a simple proposition - returning to the idea of producing things which we all need rather than producing for the greed of a few, using only those resources which can be recycled or renewed - but it feels harder than that.

It is clear that our real needs are mostly emotional and those which are material, such as the need for food and shelter or even fancy technological gadgets such as my (Micheline) powered wheelchair, could easily be met from the abundance of the earth's renewable resources if we stopped doing all the other stuff which is plundering it – and us. The pressure to keep plundering is enormous, as described in detail in this excerpt from Leon Rosselson's wonderful song: '*We Sell Everything*':

"So tell me, sir, do you prefer to be a lousy saboteur
Or help to boost that national economy?
Because production only rises and investments only boom
When the demand stimulates the supply
Then everyone will prosper so I hope it's very plain
That it's your patriotic duty to buy...
Cough drops, cricket bats, iron lungs, knickknacks
Wooden legs, wedding rings, we sell everything
Slug killers, killer slugs, road drills, ear plugs
Time bombs, tombstones, merchant banks and garden gnomes
Toothpaste, defoliants, genital deodorants
Strychnine, gasoline, benzene, polythene...
Fruit machines, magazines, baked beans, submarines
Handcuffs, face creams, pep pills and private dreams
Synthetic fibres, tranquilizers, inorganic fertilizers
Canned beer, barbed wire, dividends at five points higher
Mars bars, fast cars, Jesus Christ as Superstars
Life insurance, cigarettes, package tours and Sabre jets...
And the new supersonic fractional orbital bombardment system
That annihilates everything that moves
Within a range of 7.528 light years...

ENOUGH IS ENOUGH

Firstly, it is good to notice how the massive, daily attempts to get us to collude with capitalism don't always work:

Tim K: *"Well I don't really think I am a good consumer. I don't know if it is a gender thing but I don't really understand how advertising works. If I see something that interests me I will go and look it up to find the best version available. I don't (think) I buy things on impulse. I don't really think I am the target audience chosen by capitalism although I am ready to eat my words if you show me otherwise. My wife is* my reference so she might say she wants a new handbag and I think, 'But you've got two already. Why do you need another one?' and if I have got shirts, I don't really notice until someone tells me my shirts look terrible and I need to get rid of them. I didn't know it looked terrible!"

Micheline: "I remember, at art college, where they were trying to persuade me to get my act together if I wanted to make it in the competitive world of graphic design, that I couldn't be arsed (laughs). I thought I just don't really want the money. I don't care. It wasn't enough to get me up in the morning. I remember thinking, well I could go out and work to get the money to buy a jumper but I could just as well stay at home and knit the jumper and it would probably be nicer (laughs). I would enjoy that more. What could I get (with money) that I wanted? Not a lot!"

Alan: "My Dad, who grew up in Liverpool where he was raised as a Catholic – he saw a lot of poverty and deprivation and ultimately left. With his brother, he walked down to Birmingham to look for work in the back end of the 1930s. I think his take on the whole thing was to fight the injustice. That was what he did. That was his reaction. I think my Dad's attitude was more about improving things for everybody. And I'm like that I think. It doesn't interest me at all, you know, home improvement. I do the odd thing if it is broken but not 'improvement.' Luckily my wife is the same so it's fine."

Susan: "What do I really need? I really need to walk in the countryside, to be with friends, to be stimulated intellectually. You don't need things to do that do you?"

We are still fully human. The challenge for us all is to find ways to acknowledge and share the gifts and the riches we already have – in practical ways:

Alan: "Think of the enormous waste of natural resources that we take out of the earth to make cars. Think of the enormous waste in terms of *the human labour needed to build and maintain them. Cars could be pooled and we could use them when we need them."*

And in emotional ways:

Micheline*: "When I think about our gifts, I think about my friend M. Because of an impairment, M. can't talk. She needs a lot of attention, not all the time but quite a bit of the time. Some would question what M. can do for others but people, particularly children, just love to sit by her. They feel peaceful. They feel some feeling of acceptance or something happens when they are just close to her doing nothing, really doing nothing. You can't be with many people and do nothing and it's alright. You are with somebody that can't move or speak and they are happy, absolutely happy when you do nothing with them. That is a gift! That is something! That's such a valuable thing!"*

From Exploitation to Meaningful Work

> *"Work is love made visible. And if you cannot work with love but only with distaste, it is better that you should leave your work and sit at the gate of the temple and take alms of those who work with joy."*
> **Kahlil Gibran, from 'The Prophet'**

There is no doubt that work can be one of the most deeply satisfying aspects of our lives. It can be the expression of our creativity, of our personal values, our love for others, our connection with the natural world, our inventiveness and curiosity and our desire for intellectual challenges.

All work has value when it has some meaningful purpose, including repetitive and 'mundane' work such as the washing up or mowing the lawn. Even hard physical labour can bring a profound sense of satisfaction. However, our relationship to work can alter our experience of it. How the world values that work, and the conditions under which we have to do it, make a big difference. Childcare, for example, can be seen as nothing more than an indulgence when it is of the unpaid single-parenting kind, but the same work performed as a professional child-minder can suddenly elevate us from useless scrounger to hardworking decent human with a monetary reward and status in society. A parent may find themselves extremely isolated in their care-taking role at home, but a child-minder may be working with colleagues in a supportive environment, having a laugh whilst dividing out the play dough. The division of labour may relegate some us to such a small and repetitive component of a job that it becomes truly boring, but this is to do with how society organizes work, not the value of the work itself.

For those of us who have experienced exclusion from the labour market because of discrimination, it has made us aware that having valued work is one way we are able to feel part of our communities and part of the bigger world. It makes us feel necessary and therefore validates our existence.

Work, however, is not always the same thing as paid employment, especially under a for-profit economic system. Although this truth is virtually hidden from us, all paid work under this system is based on exploitation. By exploitation we mean taking part of the produce of our labour for purposes which are not ours.

We may be skilled carpenters for example, working for furniture making companies. We make tables and the company sells them for a price which includes the materials we used, our skills and time to make it, the overheads of the businesses and some more to put in the banks of the owners or shareholders of the companies. The owners of the businesses can use that profit for anything they wish although it was our labour which created it. We have been made to feel this is a perfectly legitimate 'return on their investment' even when they are multi-billionaires and we are still scratching around in the dirt despite working until we drop:

John: "My dad started in a boot factory in Glasgow, doing shoes and that. After the war there was no demand for stuff like that and they went bankrupt and he ended up in the shipyards. So, to get extra money he started working in pubs, you know, the weekend work. I was bought up in a flat in Glasgow, a two-bedroom flat, there were six of us there – my mother and father and four children. The highlight of our week was Sunday morning – we always had a packet of crisps. That was it. We looked forward to this packet of crisps."

Chrissie: "My dad had a full-time job, he worked for the Ordnance Survey and I guess you'd say that, at that point, he was a professional. He worked on drawing maps – a cartographer – but we were really poor. In order to make ends meet, he had to do two other jobs. He worked as a gardener and, because of his graphics skills, he used to do posters for the local United States Air Force base. He used to do posters for their bingo nights and their parties and things like that."

This is not the only aspect of exploitation we accept on a daily basis.

Alan: "One of my early experiences of exploitation was as an apprentice working in about 1968. There was a lot of 'piece work' in those days and part of the time I was in a machine shop after I came out of the Apprentice Training School.

The production jobs were all timed and you were paid according to however many components you produced. In those days, before 'Equal Pay' and all the rest of it, there were two rates for any one job – one rate was for 'Men' and the other rate was for 'Women and Youth'. So it meant that a man could make one hundred components on a machine and a woman or a youth – which I was at the time – could produce exactly the same hundred things and get an awful lot less money for it."

That was a really stark example to me and it was one of my first experiences on the shop floor when I came out of the training school. It was a raw example of economic exploitation. Theft – that's the way I see it – just the basic economic theft that goes on within the way that things are set up within our society."

Chrissie: "My mind went back to my very first job which was as a Chamber Maid and there was something very demeaning, not about the work itself, but the way I was treated by the people who employed me. One of the things that we had to do was to make sandwiches for the guests when they were going out for the day and the owner of the hotel would say, "That margarine, scrape it on and scrape it off!" and that's how I felt I was being treated, you know, with the absolute minimum of respect. Well, there wasn't any respect really. So, there's that whole thing about respect and being seen as the lowest of the low."

Jill: "Well, it feels like I was born being able to smell poverty. That's what it feels like. I think I must have been born with a tattoo across my head: 'POOR', 'cos every time I looked in the mirror I felt poor and, kind of, could see I was poor."

John: "*My mother had to look after four kids and that in a two-roomed flat, you know. She never really had any time to herself except when we were at school. The cooking facilities were the fire. We didn't have a cooker. We had an open fire with a thing at the side with kettles and that on it and one sink. We used to get the old bath and basin out to wash our feet and stuff.*
We'd be doing toast on the fire with a fork, a slice of bread with sugar on it, mince and tatties on the table. I like mince and tatties. Just as well 'cos that's all we got! We never had any roast dinners or anything like that. No sweets or deserts. It's one of these things anyway. Lots of people in Glasgow were in the same boat. It was better outside the house, meeting up with your mates and that."

As with all oppressions, the lack of value put on you by the 'world' becomes internalised. These feelings are the ones that can follow us through our lives no matter how much our material situation may improve:

Jill: "*When I looked in the mirror, I saw this very scruffy child with masses and masses of curly hair. I always had nits. You could never get a comb through my hair 'cos it was just too curly and my skin was quite dark so I just looked odd, just looked, I don't know, I must have been called ugly, I felt ugly. I felt completely ugly and worthless. Totally ugly, totally worthless and just odd - thinking I shouldn't be here and not knowing where I should be. And I remember that, like being really little and actually knowing that – not being able to articulate it and not the exact words going round in my head but just feeling so odd and so remote and so, you know, worthless and weird. Weird feeling, very little, even maybe standing on a chair – that small – to look in the mirror*"

One of the main things that makes work meaningful is that the end product is something we want, we believe in, is in accord with our own notions of right and wrong. Much paid employment is not about this at all. The end product may be no more than more sales of a particular brand of merchandise that means nothing to us. Or it may simply feed some bureaucratic machine which we don't even like with endless forms and computer files which have used up our precious mental energy to no real purpose.

Even if we manage to choose work that is more meaningful to us and has an outcome of which we can be proud, as in most public sector or voluntary sector jobs, our goodwill can also be exploited. By guilt-tripping us into accepting long and unsocial hours, low pay and often unrealistic workloads, we can suffer through financial insecurity and through the stress of trying to do a job well which cannot be done well under the conditions imposed on us.

With these socially useful jobs – nursing, teaching, support workers and so on, it is harder to see how this exploitation is caused by capitalism, but it is. Capitalism requires a fit, educated and compliant work force to do its work. It needs an education system and a health system and a criminal justice system for its own ends. It needs society's casualties to be swept out of the way or medicated so they do not disrupt things and it does not want revolution, so it also needs to confuse and placate or frighten people into thinking they are personally to blame for anything not working so it needs to control the media and the laws that govern us and it needs armies of social workers to prevent a more obvious breakdown of society. In terms of the system, most of our services are only allowed to exist if they serve capitalism's primary aim of creating profit.

In a world where the majority of people do not own their own land and where money is needed to buy the things we must have in order to survive, we can all be blackmailed very easily into taking part in this system even if we doubt it's motivation or value. Destitution is not a very appealing alternative.

It has to be said that many people do *not* doubt its motivation or value. Most of us actually think there is nothing really wrong with individuals making a profit for themselves except when a few renegades, greedy bankers for example, muck it up for the rest of us. We have so little choice and there is pleasure to be had in some of the material or status gains to be made if we can succeed, that we convince ourselves that it is okay but this is really because the price we are paying as a human race is being hidden from us – especially in the richer, western economies. Alan describes how he came to realize that profit is a huge drain on human society:

Alan: "I'd always worked in big factories, helping to make cars or parts for airplanes and they were all big places where you never saw the owners, let alone met them. We saw managers pass through the shop floor from time to time but mostly we saw their representatives – the departmental foremen who oversaw production and acted in the owner's interests at all times - even though they, themselves, may well have never met the owners of the companies.

"The role of these shop floor supervisors was often articulated with such phrases as, "We've got to keep production going at all costs. The tracks (the ever-moving conveyor belts, that moved vehicles through the assembly shop for example) must never stop!

"I remember one occasion when I worked as a labourer in a Chrysler factory, when one conveyor on which car engines were being assembled, was threatened with a stoppage by a serious water leak from a nearby burst water pipe. The foremen, all resplendent in their bright blue jackets, got a gang of us labourers to run around like blue-arsed flies fetching large bags of sawdust to soak up the leaking water and to try to stem the encroaching tide to prevent it from reaching the engine track.

"The guys working on the track were watching the water's inevitable progress with a keen interest! Us labourers worked hard. We did create an enormous sawdust mound between the leak and the engine track but to no avail! Water, being water, found the swiftest route to the doomed track. Once the water had reached its goal, the foremen

were forced, with much embarrassment, to stop the track. The guys working on the track gave up a big cheer as soon as the red stop-button was pushed and the track ground to a halt.

"Whilst the tracks were moving, profit was being generated and the owners were happy. This was the situation in many workplaces for many years.

"My father was a socialist and I'd learned from him that: part of the value of what was produced in those factories was given to workers in the form of wages; part of the value was used by the factory owners to cover the cost of their overheads (the costs they incurred in buying raw materials, powering the machinery, lighting the workshops, maintaining the machinery and so on); part of the money was invested in the company to make the company more competitive (more efficient working methods, more efficient machinery and so on) and part of the value that had been created went as profit into the pockets of the owners for their personal benefit. Company owners, politicians and others, always justified that profit, in society at large, as being completely necessary. Without it, they said, companies wouldn't have the money to re-invest, to stay competitive – to survive.

"Personally, I didn't have a problem with people investing money and becoming more efficient. It did seem a little sad that companies were constantly locked into this competitive situation which none of them seemed able to do anything about other than 'beat the opposition' and, ultimately, force their competitors out of business – making their workers unemployed in the process!

"I'd been away from factory work for many years and when I finally returned it was to a very small-scale precision engineering machine shop making very accurately produced parts for Rolls Royce aircraft and marine engines. The small company I worked in was owned by one man, who employed half a dozen of us to run the computer-controlled machinery that made the very accurate engine parts.

"The boss spent much of his time working in his office at one end of the relatively small workshop and I worked at the opposite end - next to

the workshop entrance. Every Thursday morning, around ten o'clock, the boss would put on his jacket, gather together his cheque books and I'd watch him walk the length of the workshop, past my machine, on his way out of the door to conduct his financial dealings with the local bank.

"Even though I'd understood, in some sort of theoretical sense, that company owners made profits out of their workers, it wasn't until I'd seen _this_ company owner walking down the machine shop with his cheque books tucked under his arm, that I'd realised that every second, of every minute, of every day that I worked for that boss, I was being robbed of part of the value of what I was producing – the part that he was banking as 'his' profit.

"The _amount_ of profit was hidden from me of course but I did notice that he drove a fancy car when I cycled to work on my bicycle; he had four or five holidays abroad every year when I struggled to get the money together to have one; he lived in a very posh house on the opposite side of town to me and his kids had been educated at a private school. He probably will have a fat pension whilst I will have to make do with the minimum State Pension.

"This guy was a small fish in the grand scheme of things but we have all seen the enormous houses on the edges of our big cities and those that literally cost millions scattered around England's posh village scene.

"We've seen the fancy cars dropping their children off outside the prep-schools, we've seen the private jets and helicopters at the airports and we've heard about the extraordinary amounts of money they lavish on food and drink in expensive restaurants.

"This is an enormous drain on communities all over the world because every minute of every day, the owners of every private enterprise on the planet from Amazon to McDonalds, from G4S to Tesco are stealing this enormous profit element from our labour – from every bit of work we do – enriching themselves at the expense of us and our communities."

How do we survive and stay relatively human? Well, the humaneness in us is fundamentally irrepressible. Most of the real, necessary and satisfying work which needs to be done we do voluntarily, in our 'spare' time. We raise our children, do the housework, shop, cook and dish up millions of meal a day, help out our friends and neighbours, visit people in hospital, care for our sick and elderly relatives, support our church communities, do things for charities, run all manner of groups, clubs, societies, become campaigners and local councillors, sing in choirs, plant and tend gardens and allotments, feed the birds, babysit, teach and learn from each other and listen to and comfort each other when we are distressed, bereaved or afraid. Some people even risk their lives in volunteer rescue services on the sea, mountains and overseas in war situations, just because they want to. In fact, life would not work without all this unpaid labour – not even for one day. So the notion that paid employment is what makes everything tick is a very false one.

It is clear that the more meaningful 'real' work which we get paid for, e.g. nursing, is enhanced by the humaneness of the employee, who will often add 'value' to the job as defined in the job description for which you are rewarded by money, by all manner of extra kindnesses: use of their own intelligence to solve day to day problems; humour; attention; experience and often hours of unpaid labour – 'beyond the call of duty'. This is especially true in the public and voluntary sectors where it is almost the norm. We make it work because we do not want to see the horrors that might happen if we didn't, but this also allows our goodwill to be exploited:

Carrie: "*They're takin' the piss aren't they! If you enjoy doing something and you do it to the best of your ability and you do a really good job but your not getting the recognition, you're playing above your weight and the more you do it, the more they take advantage and expect you to do it!*

You never get the payment reward or the actual recognition for doing it. I mean, I get my own pleasure and satisfaction from doing a good job, you know, but you never get the recognition for it or someone to just say, "Gosh, that was good! Well done you!" Bigger mug you for doing it, you know? That's exploitation."

A good proportion of paid employment is based on industries that are not just meaningless, but actually harmful. The market for such products is often created from our addictions, fear and insecurities or our desire for status. It is hard to know because we do not ask the question enough, what effect it has on our emotional health to submit to spending a good piece of our lives working towards ends which are destructive to people and the planet. At some level we must know that this is what we are doing but we cannot really allow ourselves to consciously feel it or we probably couldn't do it. We must find ways to not think about it or to convince ourselves that there is some good in it somewhere or the consequences of not doing it would be even more harmful, e.g. your family would starve – which may of course be true!

The poorest people do the worst sorts of work under the worst sorts of conditions. It has all come to feel so normal and unchangeable that we have almost stopped questioning the problem with exploitation and started to just think that the problem is with distribution – where the money goes and the economic inequality which is created. We think redistributing the profits alone would make everything okay, but it won't.

THE DIVISION OF LABOUR

The division of labour, which came about primarily through industrialization, has radically altered the way we work. Once, we made something from scratch to the finished article ourselves. This meant that we could see the fruits of our labour right in front of us and we could take pleasure from knowing we had achieved something. The workmanship in that 'product', be it a nicely ploughed field or a warm crusty loaf, was something in which we could take pride. For those of us lucky enough to be able to create something new, using highly developed craft skills, that pride can intensify.

The same applies to a service. Once a nurse would do nearly everything for their patient: bathing; tending to dressings; bed making; food and drink; taking temperature, pulse and blood pressure measurements using their own hands and ears and listening, comforting and explaining what the doctor meant. As technology, privatisation and the division of labour has increased, many of these tasks are done by separate teams of people: the ones who fill the water jugs; the ones who clean the wards; the ones who bring the tea and biscuits; the ones who bring and serve the meals (but don't stick around to help those who need help to eat the food); the ones who operate the mobile shop and library; the physiotherapist who get you moving again and the psychiatric team who must be called in to manage any one who shows signs of upset, like a tear or two.

MECHANISATION

Nurses, for example, are now primarily operators of machines: one to take your temperature; another to monitor your blood pressure and a third to automatically control any intravenous 'drips'. It is true that an automated personal hygiene machine has not yet been invented so nurses still need to handle peoples bodies in order to keep them clean and comfortable but for how long before 'progress' will make even the rubbery touch of the compulsory gloved hand a distant memory.

This process of the division of labour, constantly de-skills people. I remember a recent example when I explained to a nurse that the blood pressure machines don't work on me because of the unusual size and shape of my arms and I said she would have to resort to the old method of pumping up an arm-band and listening for the beats – at which point the colour drained out of her panicked face. More importantly, this sub-division of labour separates us from the reward of seeing the effectiveness of our work and, consequently, our reward increasingly comes only in the pay packet.

We are gradually disassociated from any 'higher' purpose as we don't experience the link between our community and ourselves. This is probably a factor in explaining how we can be coerced into engaging in activities with which we might disagree or believe to be worthless, destructive or inhuman – working in cigarette factories for example or making weapons of war.

Mechanisation is not always bad. It has made some work that was pure drudgery a thing of the past but it has denigrated work which relies on direct use of our hands and the kind of people who do it. We are conditioned to believe from our schooldays that there are two different types of people – those 'clever' ones who will work with their brains and those 'thicker' ones who will have to work with their hands.

The people who hold this attitude were clearly not paying attention in their human biology lessons because, if they had been, they would have grasped the fact that hands do not function independently of our brains. Likewise, footballers do not have brains in their feet. It is not even a different kind of intelligence that divides the intellectual from the craftsperson. It is just what we decide to apply our intelligence to. We can and do, all use our minds to think about ideas and to learn to handle a knife and fork.

Everything we do requires some application of intelligence and that intelligence expands in relation to the information or 'data' it is given to use. If you live all your life in a darkened room with nothing to do, you will come out of it with a very limited range of abilities. You might be diagnosed as having a low IQ or being 'backward'. If, however, you have lived a life surrounded by stimulation and opportunity you might well become a person who can: develop brilliant ideas that are admired on the world stage; creatively paint, decorate and repair your own house and play a mean saxophone in the local swing band!

The over-automation of work denies many people the necessary experience of learning through their senses and limits their ability to think for ourselves. It denies us the satisfaction of making, doing and mending with our own powers. This disassociation from our labour and the end product, leaves us feeling no sense of pride or achievement in anything other than the size of our pay packet. The reward in this 'deal' is through spending our earnings – a very poor substitute for meaningful work. It is what Karl Marx, the German philosopher, referred to as 'alienation':

> *"Everything the economist takes from you in the way of life and humanity he restores to you in the form of money and wealth"*
> ***Karl Marx***

To limit the range of 'data' our mind can use is to deprive people of something they need to develop fully. We are more used to thinking about this in terms of being deprived of higher education, reading the plays of Shakespeare, learning Latin or listening to classical music but there is now a much bigger danger of being deprived of the information we learn through our senses by direct contact with the physical world, exploring the properties of materials and tools. Humans have learned in this way for all of our history – until now. Through such learning, we learn about cause and effect, a vital component of understanding our world. People who have been deprived of his kind of learning and who have been corralled into 'ivory towers' of intellectualism and put in powerful positions of authority, have to rely on those of us who did learn through practical application, to create a functional society. Under the current upside-down system, such practical, functioning, intelligence is barely recognised and certainly not financially rewarded.

Even above and beyond this disparity between status and usefulness, is the fact that we need to make things ourselves, for our own well-being.

Matthew Crawford, an American writer in his book 'The Case For Working With Your Hands' talks about the skills needed to repair his beloved motorbikes:

> "The repairman has to begin each job by getting outside his own head and noticing things, he has to look carefully and listen to the ailing machine".

He speaks in his book of how unsuited he was to academic life in the 'knowledge economy' despite his qualifications and high salary. After six months in this role he gave it all up and, with his savings, opened up a motorcycle repair shop. He concludes his book by saying:

> "We are basically dependent beings; one upon another and each in a world that is not of our making. To live wakefully is to live in full awareness of this. To live well is to reconcile ourselves to it and try to find whatever excellence we can. For this some economic conditions are more favourable than others. When the conception of work is removed from its scene of execution, we are divided against one another and each against himself. For thinking is inherently tied up with doing and it is in rational activity together with others that we find our peculiar satisfaction. A humane economy would be one in which the possibility of achieving such satisfaction is not foreclosed ahead of time for most people." **(Penguin Books, 2009)**

Matthew's story reminds us that the system also hurts people who are supposed to be the winners – the 'privileged'. Ben describes the almost inescapable pull for the middle classes to collude with the values of capitalism however valiantly people like his parents tried to hold on to their integrity:

Ben: "For all the transformation that my parents have done and all their politics, for all the collectives that they lived in before they had us, they did, and I say this with all the love and respect in the world, they did sell out on certain principals, certain truths that they kind of acknowledged maybe when they were my age.

There's something about this system, where you feel that you don't have a choice, that's so pervasive and so potent that somehow ... I guess I have this fear that one day I will look up and I'll be like, "Oh shit! I've fucking sold out as well!"

EARLY HURTS

As children, most of us find ourselves in an unequal battle of wills with adults. Our inner drive to learn and develop in our own unique way, versus the pre-set goals of our parents, sets the scene for the rest of our lives. "Put that down!", "Eat your dinner!", "Go to bed!" – endlessly commanding us to subjugate our own desires to theirs about a hundred times a day. If we protest too much we may get hurt or punished. As soon as our desire to direct our own play is over-ridden by adults in nursery or school by forcing us to knuckle down and learn our colours, numbers or letters for purposes we have not (yet) chosen for ourselves, we are being prepared to accept a life in which our freedom to explore is curtailed and exploitation is the 'norm'.

Micheline: "From the age of about nine, I was quite obsessed with drawing – I loved it and I was very good at it. To me, it was a form of self-expression, it was like a language that you could see – to show what was inside my head.

When I got to art college, the only thing that people were interested in was how I could earn a living – via this 'thing'. So, I was directed to a graphic design course and spent months learning how to design, you know, cornflake boxes and stuff like that. That was about the last thing under the sun that I actually wanted to do."

"Even then, I was told I would never succeed at it, even if I wanted to because I had no 'competitive spirit' and if I wanted to succeed, in what was a very competitive and able-bodied world (as a disabled woman) I'd have to be twice as good as everybody else. So, unless I was really driven, I wasn't going to make it. I remember thinking that I'd rather clean floors than sell ...... I can't even explain it really. To have a skill of mine that made me so visible, was so personal, I think that's what it was, to just be used to make money, to advertise things which I had no interest in what-so-ever, was about the worst thing that I could imagine. It was like having a hand put inside your brain - my actual creative mind – to manipulate my ideas for their own ends and I actually couldn't do it so I walked away. I walked away from it with not a clue as to what I was going to do. It almost stopped me drawing. It almost took away the pleasure I had in that skill. So, it was huge! I had no language to talk about it – I couldn't tell anybody what I was feeling – it was just all inside me, you know. It was weird. It was awful actually".

We have probably just uncovered the tip of the iceberg of damage inflicted upon us by the rapid rise of a for-profit economy and its inevitable exploitation. If work is 'love made visible', most of us have to do it in our spare time. We have to try and hang on to our sense of what matters whilst being told on a daily basis that we are not working when doing these things, that during the hours we are not in paid employment, we are doing nothing, we are contributing nothing. We are scroungers, or 'useless eaters' to quote Hitler. Because our value as human beings is tied to our earning power, even when we are employed, the type of work which is primarily about meeting human needs is the lowest paid and is associated with having less intelligence - the 'unskilled labour force' (who care for people and keep us all from being buried alive in our own waste for example).

The skills and abilities to understand and manage human relationships which this kind of work requires, is becoming recognised as 'emotional intelligence'.

There is increasing pressure to earn higher salaries in jobs which are nearly impossible to do, given the time, resources and expectations attached to the position. This is leading to high levels of work-related stress, mental health problems and alcohol and drug abuse amongst professionals such as teachers, doctors and social workers:

> *"The occupations that reported the highest prevalence rates of work-related stress (three-year average) were health professionals (in particular nurses), teaching and educational professionals and caring personal services (in particular welfare and housing associate professionals)"* **Stress & Psychological Disorders in Great Britain 2013, Health & Safety Executive**

At the top of the scale can be seen almost pathological insecurities caused by the attempt to rationalize their privilege, the corruption of morals and the insatiable greed of the super-rich. Based on being separated early from the 'common people', brutalised as young people and forced to take responsibility for everything without necessarily having any ability to do so, such lives are often hall-marked by isolation and pretence. The inability to connect their actions to their results is a dangerous reflection of how separated they are from their own selves and how unfit they are to rule over others.

Meaningful Work – Production for Need Not Greed

It is worth remembering at this point that, for much of our past, work was not based on such exploitation. Although it was present to some degree in serf societies, it has only reached these epic proportions once people had their land stolen and were forced into the gaping mouth of the industrial revolution, around 400 years ago. We are only about sixteen generations away from a completely different way of life and in some places in the world, hidden in rain forests and inhospitable deserts, these ancient ways still exist.

We are perfectly capable of thinking our way out of this current phase of history into a better one. One of the first tasks must be to redefine the meaning of work, to acknowledge and value the reality of our unpaid labour, to understand the harmful nature of exploitation and how it is an inevitable part of the capitalist system and to construct paid employment – at least whilst we still have a moneyed economy – which creates the conditions under which we can produce for our needs without exploitating each other or the earth's finite resources.

A start would be refusing to describe those of us who work voluntarily, not as 'unemployed' but as 'unpaid' instead. After all, just imagine what might happen if we stopped doing this work…

The Day the Unpaid Workers Went On Strike

Imagine one day when all the voluntary workers decide to go on strike. What would happen?

It is seven in the morning and no mothers are up cooking breakfast and helping children to get washed and dressed. No homework is found and no packed lunches are packed. Dads are waking up to hear hungry children raiding the kitchen, babies crying in their full nappies, dogs and cats scrabbling at doors. Can they just leave this and go to work? No. They phone the grandparents "Mum! Dad! You've got to come and get the kids up, Flossie has gone on strike!" But to their horror, their grandparents are out playing bowls and clipping the hedge – they're on strike too!

Many elderly and disabled people are phoning the emergency services, or opening the front door and wandering out into the street in their pyjamas. Their carers have gone to the park for a spot of sun-bathing. Dogs are running in and out of the traffic which is slowly grinding to a halt.

By lunch-time, most men and children are hungry. Queues at the sandwich bar and fast-food joints are stretching down the road and cafes have run out of food. By evening, with no hot meal waiting in the family home, bizarre meals are being concocted from fridge leftovers and store cupboards. But who will do the shopping to replace it?

A 'State of Emergency' is rapidly declared and the Army, Social Services and even the Civil Service are requisitioned to life-saving activities, setting up feeding stations for children and the elderly, taking children to and from school, supplementing the Home Care Service twenty-four hours a day, and even organising state laundry services. Many more people have to be employed and trained to care for each other.

Imagine this goes on for weeks and months. What would happen? Thousands of large and small charities, left without trustees and management boards, would have to close down.

Schools would be left without governing bodies and would soon become unable to function in a democratic way.

People receiving calls to jury service would throw them in the bin. The legal system would no longer function, as courts were closed and people on remand remained on remand for evermore.

Blood and organ donors would stop donating. Most surgeries would soon be affected and soon the Health System, as we know it, would cease to function. People would be selling their blood and organs to the highest bidders.

Thousands of clubs, societies, campaigns and support groups would cease to function.

Local members of all political parties would stop meeting, leaving their paid representatives isolated and without a mandate. The parliamentary system would break down, as would local government, having no more direct connection with the public. Even the National Lifeboat Service would no longer set out to rescue sailors in distress.

It's clear that capitalism or any other system, could not work without a massive input of unpaid labour. Without this labour people would die of neglect and none of our institutions could continue to operate for long.

There is nothing wrong with doing good things voluntarily, of course. What is wrong is the complete lack of recognition of the necessity of this work to the functioning of society or the acknowledgement that the economic system exploits this labour too – not just that of those in paid work. In other words, the labour force consists of both paid and unpaid workers and the unpaid workers are the ones which keep it all going but are told they are doing NOTHING.

The 'scrounger' rhetoric used to demonise people who do not get paid for their labour, lone parents in particular, feeds into an even bigger misconception. We are told that the poor are dependent on the state and that even with all the profits made by industry, our taxes and our national insurance contributions, the state still cannot afford to meet our basic needs. The reality is the opposite. 'The poor' do all the work to produce the wealth and are then forced to subsidise the rich. The rich depend completely on the poor to keep them in their exalted positions.

When many of us try to imagine the end of capitalism and it's replacement with an alternative, pictures of bloody revolutions followed by chaos and a rapid decline into anarchy tend to spring to mind. Thoughts of failed attempts at communism, tanks, Che Guevara, Stalin, night arrests and years of hard labour in an icy gulag for voicing the wrong opinion dampen our enthusiasm and send us running to the nearest Costas for a quick cup of capitalist comfort. We think that it is too different, too difficult, too unimaginable, to ever become a reality.

What would a system look like which was based on producing what people need without making a profit? How could it possibly work?

The amazing thing is that we are already doing it. We have already worked out how to answer most people's basic needs, leading to us spreading and colonising most of the world and dominating all other living species.

Not only do we happily donate our labour outside of the economic system, we have set up public services, public housing, public utilities, worker co-operatives and a multitude of not-for-profit charities and campaigns, artists collectives, co-housing communities, bartering systems, self-help religious and cultural centres, all of which employ many millions of people on a global scale and which do not entail private ownership. Why is it not possible to expand this sector of our organised world until it dominates? Is there anything we need which could not be produced this way?

I, (Micheline) for example, need a powered wheelchair to move around and live a life under my own control. I *could* stay alive without it. That is true but I would be completely dependent on the availability and willingness of other people to facilitate my every move and, in my experience, other people can usually find something else they would rather be doing. Now, the capacity has been developed to aid my autonomy by technical means, I think most people would agree that this would be *useful* production, a good application of our inventiveness and resources. Could my chair be produced by a workers' co-operative? Yes it could! Could the raw materials it requires be mined, smelted or reclaimed from scrap by people working in a worker-owned co-op? Yes they could! Could it be maintained by similar groups of engineers? Yes it could!

It *could* but would it? This makes me have to face another fear. Would anyone give a shit about whether I could get myself out of bed in the morning if they could not see a way to profit from answering my need? We are constantly made to feel the answer would be no. We are force-fed every day a version of ourselves that proclaims our selfishness – our overriding desire to gain something.

At election time, for example, the whole population of the UK is asked to decide who to elect on the basis of 'Under which party will I, personally, be better off?' i.e. we should exercise our democracy on the single criteria of the size of our bank balance. Well, in my life, it is true that I have met people who are apparently primarily motivated by the hope of personal gain but I have had far more experience of being on the receiving end of generosity and kindness. In fact if I hadn't been picked up and dusted down by many a passing stranger, I'm not sure I would still be alive to write this book. And likewise, I have done a fair bit of acting for the benefit of others rather than myself. So, I would be prepared to risk facing that particular fear. I am able to believe that if someone was offered the job making powered wheelchairs, for a living wage, which would automatically be provided for people who needed them, who's quality of life would be dramatically improved and from which no one would be raking off a profit, he or she would be delighted to go to work every day and return home at night with a deep sense of satisfaction. The employees of the company I actually use already do this I'm sure. I meet them and talk to them. I am absolutely sure their job satisfaction would only grow if they knew they were not also funding the owners, or shareholders of the enterprise. Their products could be more affordable or their productivity could improve by not having some of the value they create siphoned off into someone's private stash.

What about the original investment? Why would anyone put money into a new business if they didn't expect a 'return' on their money? Why take the risk? Well, we invest in schools and hospitals without worrying about this so why not have the same approach to the answering of other needs? If we, as a democratic community, decide our real needs are 'A, B and C', then it would be a logical progression to create the 'machinery' to organise the production of 'A, B and C'.

How can we help each other get from here to there? Our first step must be recognizing the true value of unpaid and low-paid work and the people who do it, including us. We can bestow respect and status on whoever we like regardless of the size of their bank balance. We can call everything we do which makes our home, community or world a little better our 'Work' and be proud of it. We can stop using the term 'unemployed' and start describing ourselves as unpaid workers. We can appreciate our families, friends and neighbours for their contribution to the common good, knowing they will probably not recognize it for themselves:

Micheline: "As I was coming home from the shops one day recently, I was stopped by a neighbour whom I recognised only by sight. 'I just wanted to tell you something' she said, 'How much my sister and I enjoy your window boxes when we walk past your place. They are so colourful and carefully done. Our Mum died recently and we have been feeling very sad but your flowers cheer me up every time I see them. Thank you'. 'Thank you for telling me' I said, feeling instantly cheered up myself"

From Oppression to Empowerment

The fact that we oppress each other is not exactly a new idea for most of us. Women, black people and gay people for example, have been fighting for equality for hundreds of years and are still. Many of these struggles have been documented in much more depth than we could possibly manage in this book. However, there are three specific areas of oppression that are less well understood in their significance to the overall task of healing the hurts of capitalism.

The Universal Oppression of Young People – Adultism

Rich or poor, black or white, male or female, we were all once children – helpless and dependent on the adults in whose care we had no choice but to be. For some, it has meant being cared for with great love and tenderness. For some, less lucky ones, it has meant being subjected to violence, neglect and abuse. For most, it has been a mixture of both.

Children in almost all cultures and classes are not treated with the same respect as adults:

Alan: "*I wasn't so much treated as a new human being by the adults around me but as a 'child'. As a child I would have been afforded less control over my life. I would have had less opportunities to influence events in my life from what I ate; when I went to bed; when I got up; who I played with; when I played with other children; when I went shopping; when I visited my relatives and so on.*"

In many nations it is legal to beat children where it would be a punishable offence to beat an adult in the same manner. Children are 'done to' with very few rights of their own and no means of representing their own interests. Whatever situation we are born into, we just have to grin and bear it until we are grown up. It is during these early formative years that the irrationalities around us seep into our minds and form a distorted lens through which we experience the world – not just how we intellectually understand it but how we *feel* about it and ourselves.

This happens before we have enough information to analyse or question. The messages become internalised, especially the negative ones. Even when we become adults and are able to see and understand much more, these early hurts are still inside us waiting to be triggered by any situation which reminds us enough of the 'first time'.

For almost all children, even those from extremely privileged backgrounds, some of these early hurts include feeling disrespected and powerless in the face of adult control. Not many children really get listened to. Apart from the internal family messages (e.g. "You are a naughty girl") there is the 'wallpaper' of society's norms and values ('poor people deserve less', 'women are less intelligent than men', 'Jews have big noses' and so on). These messages are more insidious because they may not ever be spoken. The messages are just there – the 'reality' we must accept without question. Because they are not true, but transmitted to us as if they were, they also hurt us but more like a poisoned gas than a slap on the face.

The problem is that even when we grow up and learn better, our emotional reactions are still attached to these early, founding experiences and our consequent behaviour does not always relate to our logical thinking, especially when it relates to ourselves:

Jill: *"We were poor to the extent of not really having much to eat which gave me a lifelong thing about food which, actually, I'm just about getting over – just about now, with this fast diet. Just about getting over eating too much 'cos I'm still completely fearful of getting none tomorrow – which is completely irrational. I know it's irrational but I still do it."*

We all know for example grown men and women who are still searching for the unconditional love they never got from their mums when they were little, despite knowing full well they are not going to find it now. We also all know and probably experience ourselves, a sense of powerlessness in the face of irrationality. It is a powerlessness that is not *real* but it stops us challenging things we know are wrong.

CLASSISM

It is still difficult to persuade many people that there is only one race – the human race – although the human genome project finally proved this without doubt.

Combating racism isn't about arguing for equality amongst the different 'races' but giving up the belief in inherited racial differences at all. Similarly combating classism, which seeks to justify the exploitation of one group of people by another through notions of inherited intelligence or moral superiority, requires us to give up any belief in such genetic differences.

This false belief, that there are genetically different types of people, whilst without biological basis, was and still is, a very useful tool in any hierarchical society that needs to justify exploitation and inequality.

In our era the Eugenics Movement has hugely shaped our false perceptions about ability, intelligence and morality. Eugenics is a pseudo-science claiming that human beings come in different qualities or 'stock'. Peasants are at the bottom of the stock rating and the aristocracy are at the top. Members of the British Eugenics Society believed that certain 'stock' should not marry or inter-breed because the lower stock, having animal passions and no self-control or morals, would out-breed the 'good, thrifty and intelligent stock' (themselves) leading to a lowering of intelligence in the overall population. If this sullying of the population was allowed to continue in an uncontrolled manner, Britain would no longer be 'great'. Eugenicists were behind the: forced sterilizations of countless thousands of poor women all over Europe and eventually in the Americas; IQ testing and the mass institutionalization of disabled people. Its logic led ultimately to Hitler's 'Final Solution'. Closely tied to racist ideology, these ideas still distort our understanding of the world to this day.

All the differences of identity, apart from those we choose ourselves, are creations of the oppressive society, used to divide and rule. And 'all' means everybody, even the rich. It is vital for us to understand that the system is our problem, not its human victims:

Alan: *"Prior to getting to know 'J' and her life story, I viewed owning class people as people who, when the revolution came, would probably be put up against the nearest wall and shot. By listening to her tell the story of her early life and struggles I came to realise that youngsters who had the misfortune of being born into owning class families were routinely treated very oppressively indeed.*

"I have learned from my connections with owning class people that the separation from their families that many of them experience (often through being sent away from home to boarding schools at a very young age) has a very detrimental impact on their picture of reality."

Ben, who was raised as a middle class child, spoke about the effect on him of classism:

Ben: *"There is something damaging about a system that's so unequal because that has then served as a barrier between me and other people in my life. I think that was really apparent when I was younger - when I was a younger teenager. My parents moved to Islington which is a funny old part (of London). You've got these big old Georgian houses and some really deprived and rough estates as well, right up against each other. I really felt how polarised it was as a kid growing up – partly because I got attacked a lot. So, a consequence of the whole system that I'm talking about is that, there was such a division between the kind of privileged, middle class kids in that area and the kids who* *were living on the estates right next to where I lived, so, I was definitely targeted and singled out and battered – a few times! I walked around in fear a lot as well for some years in my teenage life, so that hurt."*

Pandora's story shows how both extremes of the class system can be experienced by just one person:

Pandora*: "You ask how capitalism has affected my family? I have two families. I'm adopted. One family is from Paraguay and they are defined by their poverty. The rest of the families around them have something – a bit of land, a chair, something like that. My family had nothing, absolutely nothing, so they put me up for adoption and I was adopted into a wonderfully upper-class family in Chelsea. So, I have two families on the global extremities of what is defined through this system, through capitalism. I liked that you talked about blame. That was a really interesting thing for me. That it's nothing to blame.*

(Alan had talked about not blaming individuals – the fault was the system.)

"Because when I'm in the Chelsea side of my life no one is causing any harm. Everyone has the best intentions. It's just as simple as, "Everything's fine over there. Let's not make a scene." "If everyone just keeps themselves nice and polite and with a public persona, everything will be fine".
"Obviously it's not like that but it's all with very, very good intentions. But then I go to Paraguay and see my family and it's another story. It's the story of not having land. Paraguay is land. Paraguay is the land that funds and fuels all the animals in China that feed the Europeans in a cheap, mass way which is raw, industrial capitalism, defining this planet and feeding this planet as we know it. So the effects of Capitalism on both sides are right at the forefront and present and I can see it."

Classism is rarely understood or talked about in the same way as we talk about sexism or racism. It is easier to talk about 'class equality' because by doing so we can avoid the messy and uncomfortable business of examining how we treat each other – in ways which reflect our comparative privileges and prejudices. For example, people who have been to university are not good at asking people who left school at sixteen what they think. Why is this?

The Installation of Class Role Distress Patterns

In order to try to sustain capitalism, each class needs to install certain distress patterns in their children:

Those of us who were raised working class were heavily encouraged to believe that:

- The contributions that we make to society warrant a lower status

- We are inferior to other people – people who are 'failures' do working class jobs and that the work that we do is of less value than other people's work (the real value of our work is denied)

- We lack the intelligence and the ability to think, that other classes of people have

- We deserve nothing better than our allotted place in society and that we are powerless to change the social relations within society

- Other working class people (rather than the capitalist system) are responsible for our problems

- Ultimately, our salvation lies in 'getting out' of the working class by following a successful pathway through the higher education system

- We should comply with the wishes of our 'betters' and we should look for leadership outside of our own class

PEOPLE WHO ARE RAISED MIDDLE CLASS:

- Experience love as something that is conditional on doing well or doing better than others

- Are lured into fulfilling their prescribed class roles with the promise of the material rewards that compliance brings

- Experience being corrected (groomed) all the time

- Are not encouraged to contemplate failure

- Are taught to appear knowledgeable and in charge – whatever the reality of the situation is

- From early in their lives, they are sheltered from learning about the lives of working class people; are kept away from 'bad' areas and the children who live in them and are left oblivious to the reality of the oppression (i.e. its physical and emotional impact) on working class people's lives both at home and in the workplace

- End up feeling privileged but guilty

- Are groomed for professionalism – taught to separate their heart from their head – to be 'objective' and 'dispassionate'

- Have an expectation of a level of comfort and status and that higher education is the norm and is their right

- Get practice at leading and managing from an early age

- Are schooled to have a disdain for labour; are unaware of their dependence on the working class and are encouraged to deny their working class roots

- Are typically self-righteous – ultimately, they blame the poor for their poverty and bad behaviour (weaknesses)

- Design systems and write rulebooks to help them maintain their role within society (they often learn to rely on these instead of on their judgement)

- Are told they should be charitable towards others who are 'less fortunate' than themselves

- Are told that they are superior to working class people and are taught to be beholden to owning class people

OWNING CLASS PEOPLE ARE:

- Groomed for leadership from birth

- Separated out and have their emotional bonds with their loved ones broken early

- Taught to be able to stand alone and lead from a position of isolation

- Given access to the 'best' of everything

- Denied access to the things that money can't buy (love, closeness and connection)

- Taught that individual failure brings shame to their whole class

- Instilled with a powerful sense of duty

- Raised to be knowledgeable about facts and figures but not about the rational needs of human beings

- Given the message that they do not need to be clever but they do need to be charming, good at sports, the arts, hosting meals and parties and flower arranging

- Taught to manipulate people (make the decisions, give orders etc)

- Trained to use a tone of voice that makes what they are saying sound right even when it's not

- Taught that they are superior to middle and working class people

The Link Between Language and Thinking

The ability to *think* is compromised across *all* classes of people by the installation of distress patterns.

In Britain, we have a particular problem because of the issue of class-based accents. A person's social class is normally immediately identifiable by the way someone speaks. Working class people are thought to not speak 'properly' and to be unintelligent – as are people with strong regional accents. These are often seen as funny or mimicked by people who want to represent people who they consider stupid.

Middle class children are taught the 'Queen's English' and owning class children are brought up to speak with a particular accent of their own. Because of this, how they speak is a big issue for all children with much criticism and correcting of pronunciation; criticism for the use of swear words, slang and so on. Many people feel they have to lose their working class or regional accents in order to be taken seriously. Just the sound of a 'posh' (middle or owning class) voice can be very re-stimulating for working class people and it can stop them thinking.

Language skills are very important in order to develop thinking skills. We use language inside our heads to think. Unlike some instinctive skill, like learning to walk, the acquisition of language is dependent on resources. There is unequal resource amongst the different class groups for the development of language, right from infancy when some children will get spoken to, read to and listened to much more than others. This will often be reinforced at school by differences in access to school trips and journeys, access to books and computers, private coaching, travel and involvement in debates and the discussion of ideas. This will make people appear more or less intelligent. They will have differing abilities to express themselves.

Working class people often have the knowledge without the language to express it. This will affect what they are allowed to study. If you cannot reach a certain level of articulation you will be expected to make a living with your 'hands' – not your mind (you don't need to refine your language skills to do that).

Working class people defend themselves physically (fighting) whilst middle class people have been taught to defend themselves verbally (arguing) which society promotes as more civilised. This reinforces each class' attitudes of superiority and inferiority.

Mental Health System Oppression

"We don't have a mental health system - we have a mental illness system". **Christine Wilson**

Prescriptions for anti-depressants have soared all over the rich world. In some counties, such as the USA, 10% of the entire population are now taking them. Children too, some as young as three, are increasingly being medicated without their consent. In England alone,

Ritalin prescriptions for the controversial diagnosis of Attention Deficit Hyperactivity Disorder (ADHD) have quadrupled in a decade, reaching 661,463 in 2010. *(NHS business services authority 2012)*

As the hurts of capitalism have accumulated and the inequality between rich and poor has grown to epic proportions, we have become profoundly anxious as a people. Apart from the prescribed drugs, it is hard to find an adult who does not self-medicate with alcohol, tobacco, 'weed' and other so called 'recreational drugs' (especially young people) in order to cope with life.

The obvious problem, in a capitalist sense, is that drugs make huge profits for the massive pharmaceutical companies such as Glaxo Kline Smith, so they have a vested interest in our unhappiness and our vulnerability to chemical addiction. This is just as true for manufacturers of cigarettes and alcohol.

A more subtle but equally harmful aspect of the NHS is the pathologising of our anger or indeed any strong feelings at all. Too many tears, too much raging, too much trembling, are seen as symptoms of something abnormal, from the 'terrible two's' onwards. Because they are signs of something abnormal, we are told, we need experts to label them and treat them with medication or therapy. We, ordinary people, cannot help ourselves for free. We must pay professionals to do it.

Even without drugs we are pretty numb. We have to be in order to manage life as it is because 'as it is' is so far away from what we really need. We are numb and when that numbness starts to melt and uncomfortable feelings rise up, we get scared of them.

It is true that left alone and without a safe space to explore and give 'vent' to these feelings, they can be unbearable. They can lead to self-harm or even suicide. But there is a source of help, free and all around us – each other!

HEALING IS A NATURAL ABILITY

Let Me Cry

I have just come into the world
And I need to cry
I need to cry long and loud
I need to recover from my journey here
Struggles you will never know
I need to howl and scream
Not for what is ahead
Or for what is now
But for all that was behind

I entered a world full of history
Broken hearts, forgotten dreams,
Fights, pain, loss and damage
Fears and disappointments
I can see them in your eyes
Behind the love

The legacy of misguided actions,
Oppression, suppression and war
Unhealed and passed on intact
From one generation to the next
And so on down the line
I see it in your eyes
And if I am not to have to look away
Let me cry for us all

Don't try to stop me
Like you were stopped
With dummies and distractions,
Shouts and threats,
Shakes and violence
Until the fear of your reaction
Teaches me to crush myself
Into a silent ball of pain

This pain will poison my mind
Chill my heart
Block out the present
Make me ill
Stop me thinking
Make me afraid
Of my own feelings
Leaving me small and impaled
Condemned to eternally search for a Someone
Who knows
I need to cry

If you let me cry,
Stay with me and welcome my tears
I can dissolve a thousand years of grief
Keep ownership of my mind
Notice the love still in your eyes
The gentleness of your touch
Your efforts to remain close
Your hope reborn with me

I will feel the joy of living
In a breathtaking world of beauty
Amongst peoples of awesome courage
Yearn to live each moment well
Holding nothing back

And when I become an adult
And you yourself are in need
I will be able to hold you
Whilst you cry
Remind you of your goodness
Thank you for all you have done
Forgive your imperfections
Caress your aged body
Look deep into your eyes
Be still and quiet
Beside you and with you
For as long as you need me to
I will let you cry
Micheline Mason, April 2007

We humans have an inbuilt mechanism for healing from all sorts of hurts, physical or emotional and this mechanism is automatic. Watch any small child from anywhere in the world and they all behave in the same way when they are hurt. They look around for a familiar face or pair of arms, reassure themselves that they are not alone and start to howl. Or maybe just come over for a quick cuddle. Or maybe they come and tell you, very animatedly, what just happened that they didn't like. Or maybe they have a tantrum. Or maybe a shared giggle will do. Then, if they are lucky enough to find a calm and sympathetic listening ear, the display of emotion will come and go like a rainstorm, the sun will come out, a smile will reappear and the event that caused the upset will fade into memory and the child will turn back out to face the world undeterred. This is how resilient we are when we are allowed to be.

The problems only occur when something stops this process happening. Either there is no sympathetic listening ear or there is no time or people misunderstand what is happening and interfere in well-meaning but unhelpful ways – such as sticking a dummy in a child's mouth or distracting them in order to stop them crying. When this is the case, something not good happens to us. It is as if the upsetting incident gets 'recorded' including everything about it, smell, sounds, taste, sensations with the feelings it evoked at the time such as fear and this recording gets saved in a special place in our brain – a place of 'easy access' so that when something similar happens again, those recorded memories, including the feeling of fear, will be played again in the hope that *this* time the conditions will be right to allow the healing process to work.

When the recording is 'playing' it can feel to us like the original incident is happening again, right now and we will, to some degree, be driven to behave as we did back then when it first happened. This is the phenomena of the human distress pattern. It is an explanation for our human irrationality or why we do not always act on what we *know* but on what we *feel* and those two things can be completely different.

The good news is that it is never too late to start the healing process. In fact, we do continually use our own resources and each other, to try to recover from past injuries, physical or emotional. If we didn't we would probably have blown ourselves up several times over by now. We do already talk, laugh and weep our way through life, using the scraps of attention we find as we stumble through. We are 'hard-wired' to do this from birth.

Unfortunately this is made much harder for us because the process of healing is confused with the hurt itself – "Oh, don't upset yourself dear!" – and discouraged by distraction, embarrassment or even drugs. And, because we all have this backlog of things to recover from, put in the 'easy access' part of our minds just waiting for the listening ear we long for, we are not as good as we think we are at listening to other people. In fact what passes for a normal conversation is often two people waiting for the other to stop talking so they can jump in with whatever comes to 'mind' when the other person is trying to tell us something. If any of us actually gets to the end of a complete thought, a small miracle has occurred.

'ATTENTION'

Much of the world is using this word at the moment. Mostly it is in relation to school children, especially little boys. Apparently there is an 'epidemic' of a new disorder called Attention Deficit Hyperactivity Disorder or ADHD, sweeping the classrooms of the modern world, causing children to move around and make a noise when they should be sitting still and doing their sums. Drug companies are making millions of pounds (or dollars) by selling drugs such as Ritalin to doctors who sedate such children so they cause less of a problem to their harassed teachers and parents.

Well, we do believe there is such a deficit disorder but we think it is the adults who have the deficit, not the children. The children are deprived of the attention they need rather than not having enough attention for their lessons.

For example, if adults paid attention to children, they might notice that many children need to move around in order to think or learn, especially the little ones. They might notice that the rise in the number of prescriptions for Ritalin seems to mirror the rise in the use of standardised testing in schools. They just might notice this and review their practices, thereby miraculously curing thousands of 'sick' children.

So what is this thing called 'attention'? It is more than just looking someone in the eye whilst they talk, although that helps. It is a really deep, dynamic form of concentration, bringing to bear all you know about the person you are focusing on, plus holding in mind everything else which might be relevant, whilst keeping yourself mostly quiet. It is about having respect for, expectations of and curiosity about, the other person. It is about creating a safe space for the focus person to express their own thoughts and feelings without fear of criticism, or judgement.

When we can muster up this sort of attention, even just for a few minutes, it seems to allow the focus person to use their own mind in a different way to usual. It seems to allow them to use their natural healing processes to undo confusions, pain, fear or just unlock their creativity and joy in life. In this sense 'attention' is a hidden 'power' of our minds — one we all have but which we know little about. It can be developed through practice and through using the attention of others to clear out our own backlogs of 'distresses'. These pull on our attention all the time, making concentration hard and the desire to interrupt and 'tell' people almost irresistible.

The reason it is important for us all to recognise the phenomena of the distress pattern is that unless we do, we will be driven to re-create all the difficulties we now face in any new organisational or political structure, however good, because we cannot change our behaviour to make the new ideas work.

We are still learning a great deal about that which we call 'mental illness', and how to help people who are overwhelmed by their distresses, but we are certain that in a world organised around real needs, including the need for non-judgemental attention from the people who are about us, very, very little of the edifice we call the 'Mental Health System' would be required.

EMPOWERMENT

There are hopeful signs in the world that in terms of these three issues – adultism, classism and mental health, the worst may be over. In our (Alan and Micheline) lifetime – the last 64 years (since 1950) – many more people are talking about their inner lives to each other and it has become far more culturally acceptable to show your feelings – even men cry in public now.

Some children are treated with more respect than others by their parents and carers; schools are less based on terrorising their pupils with the threat of corporal punishment and child and youth participation programmes are slowly developing all over the world implementing Article 12 of United Nations Convention on the Rights of the Child:

"Every child who has a view has the right to express this view freely, in all matters affecting the child"

The Inclusive Education Movement has helped draw in marginalized and excluded children out of the shadows of segregation into the light of mainstream provision and there are movements and campaigns everywhere to protest against the exploitation of children through sexual abuse, child labour, child soldiers and such barbaric practices as female genital mutilation. The assumption that the owning class have attained their position through their superior intelligence and morality is now laughed at widely.

We are slower to realise that people in the working class are not there because they are 'thick and can't behave' and we are gradually increasing our awareness of how classism works.

In order to reclaim our power as human beings we need to:

•   Fight for our minds against exploitation by legal and illegal drug manufacturers and dealers – starting with our own addictions.

- Refuse to label our unhappiness or anger as anything other than rational grief and indignation ('Sad – not mad').

- Make space to listen to each other's life stories, especially our early years, to help us understand where many of our present life struggles are rooted and to start to leave behind the feelings of powerlessness they left embedded in our psyches.

- Understand that working class people struggle with feelings of self-doubt, fear of speaking out, denial of information available to middle and owning classes, fear of humiliation and the exhaustion caused by dealing with the 'daily grind'.

- Recognise that there are significant, but different struggles for people who are raised middle or owning class. Our class conditioning is deliberately designed to divide us and to prevent us from seeing our common humanity:

> "The class system isn't fair on them either, poor little sods, packed off to school, weaned on privatised maternity shopped in from a northern spinster. Trying to find love in the tangle of dismantled family. No one can be happy imbibing a poisoned brew. It's poisonous for us all. They'll be grateful when we unlock them from their opulent penitentiaries, they'll be grateful when their fallow lands and empty chambers feed the hungry and house the poor. They know contentment cannot be enjoyed when stolen. They need the revolution as much as we do. **Russell Brand, 'Revolution'**

Making friends across the class divide is always a good start.

From Violence to Love

"Do you want a smack?"

"No Mum"

"Well, DO WHAT YOU ARE TOLD THEN!"

The little scenario above typifies the relationship between the powerful and the oppressed. Oppressive relationships like this have probably existed for many eras before ours and the foundations for these relationships are always laid down in childhood.

No human being is born with the desire to act violently towards other human beings. Further, before anyone can act violently or can even threaten to act violently towards others, they have to have been emotionally scarred by violence – they either have to have witnessed violence or someone has to have acted or threatened to act violently towards them.

Unfortunately capitalism is a system based on violence. It was built by enslaving people, colonising many, many countries in the world, subjugating many of the world's peoples and stealing natural resources from the four corners of the earth. Capitalism can only function through exploitation and this exploitation is facilitated by the installation of the fear of violence and ultimately the actual use of violence to crush decent.

However, using overt violence against the 'masses' does not look good when trying to promote the system as fair, just and for the long-term benefit of the 'workers'. It is much better to gradually persuade people to comply with the demands of capitalism without putting up a fight or even questioning it.

We are born tiny and at the mercy of adults including the adults who are meant to protect us. To keep the wheels of capitalism turning it is essential that adults teach children to respect and be afraid of authority as soon as possible. This is done through thousands of small acts of violence by adults towards children, usually accepted by the culture as 'normal' or necessary, such as the 'smack' policy described above.

Some acts of violence are subtle and often go unrecognised:

Alan: *"When I think of an early memory of violence a particular image comes into my mind. I've got this photograph of me as quite a young tot really - not very old and I'm standing there with this pear in my hand – a piece of fruit – and there's a tear. There's a funny look on my face and there's this tear trickling down my cheek which makes it kind of bizarre, you know, it's not like a fun-packed image, you know what I mean? ...... (laughs) ...... it's not like, "Oh, look, Alan's having a good time, let's take his picture!". Something pretty weird was going on before someone took that picture! And something pretty weird was going on as they took the picture. To me, it sort of screams of 'alone' really (fighting back the tears), it's a picture of a hurt little boy who's by himself! So, what the hell was going on – for the person taking the picture? When they took that picture – I've no idea! ...... (laughs) ...... but it's a weird bloody photograph! Sometimes I look at it and I think, you know, ... (laughs and almost cries) ...... 'Why would you want to photograph that?'*

"And I know, later, my uncle (who I think took the photo), he'd be doing something bloody weird, you know and I don't have any memories of being defended by either me mother or me father. I don't remember anybody challenging him – his weirdness, you know. I don't remember anybody challenging him. Which is odd in a way 'cos my dad would argue with him a lot – about politics – he'd challenge his politics til the cows come home. That uncle often seemed to be doing strange, humiliating, unhelpful things around us as kids, you know.

Some memories of violence are of genuine but misguided attempts to protect children from pain:

Bev: "*When I was about five years old, my Mum and Dad had a pub and they had lots of people working for them in the pub. It was in the City of London and we had an aunty and uncle, Aunty Doris and I didn't really see Aunty Doris anywhere, I couldn't see her and I kept saying to Mum, particularly Mum, 'Where's Aunty Doris?' and she said, 'Oh, don't worry darling, she's gone on holiday.' OK, time went by and I was only five and my concept of time was a little bit, you know, it was what it was – I was five years old. I kept asking her where Aunty was and eventually she said, 'Oh, sit down darling, I've got something to tell you' and she told me that Aunty Doris had died – she'd had cancer and she'd died.*

"I was really shocked because I'd kept imagining her on holiday and I thought she was going to come back soon – I really thought she'd be back soon! She was like my favourite aunty. She wasn't really an aunty but she was like a family friend and I was really devastated that Mum hadn't, that she hadn't told me the truth.

"So, in my mind, that's a kind of violent thing to do because she gave me hope that I'd see her again but I never saw her again and I carried that with me, I suppose, for quite a long time. Thinking about it, I think Mum did it to protect me and in those days I think it was more of 'you didn't tell children everything' but I'd rather she'd told me the truth and then I wouldn't have had to think about her coming back. I think I felt totally bereft and I felt betrayed"

Most adults do not want to hurt children but adults have been hurt themselves and it is very difficult not to pass this on – especially when we are tired, stressed and isolated. We therefore learn early, in a personal way, that there is violence around and it is not a good thing to attract to ourselves because it hurts. We learn also that we can be violent ourselves despite our best intentions not to be. In fact violence is the rumbling background threat to everything in our lives. There is no oppression from which the ultimate threat of violence is absent.

The power of violence in not always in its actuality. Even for those of us who grow up in relative safety and security, it is the *fear* of violence that traps us in an invisible cage, unnecessarily limiting nearly every aspect of our lives:

Linda: *"I don't have a direct memory of my dad hitting my brother for example but my Mum tells me that he did. I don't have a direct memory of this little boy downstairs, you know, but I've seen a picture of him with a black eye and my Mum's told me the story about his black eye and how his dad used to hit him, in fact, she told us those stories when we were quite young… and then there's living in a house with two other families and one of them was a violent guy who used to beat his kid and I must have been …….. I was under three …… I might have been under two …… so I would have heard it 'cos it was a tiny little house.*
We went to look at it recently, it was in Battersea, a tiny little house, just two floors, we lived upstairs and they lived downstairs and he was walloping his wife and kids! His child wasn't supposed to play with us, you know, the father wanted to keep them apart so that he could just carry on doing what he was doing and nobody would challenge it. Of course, I didn't challenge it – I was two years old! (giggles) But anyway, I think it set up a lot of fear in me and it just trickled on."

It's not possible to grow up in this society without being subjected to many, many experiences of witnessing violence. When we witness violence or when someone acts or threatens to act violently towards us, we get hurt. When we are close to violence we always get hurt emotionally:

Rose: *"It definitely started at my first boarding school which I went to when I was about five and it was a special school for disabled kids. I was very good at escaping trouble, escaping punishment but I seem* *to create it for other people (laughs) and I remember – boys especially – getting hit for things that I'd kind of initiated somehow but I was too clever to get caught myself but somehow I led them into getting caught."*

"On one occasion, there was a bowl of fruit on the sideboard and I thought it would be quite good to take some grapes! I knew it was wrong, that we'd have to ask permission or whatever so I took a couple of grapes and so did my friend Peter, who I'm still friends with actually, sixty years later but, of course, he got caught. A staff member came in while he was taking his grapes and he got thrashed – the backs of his legs were slap, slap, slap! Course, I ended up feeling guilty about that and feeling outraged that, just for stealing some grapes, he had to get slapped like that!

"Then another time, we were in class and there was this other little boy called David Fleming, I still remember him and he was sort of sitting next to me but over the other side of the isle kind of thing and I looked at him and he was showing me his willy ...... (laughs) ...... and he was kind of indicating to me to show him mine you see, which I did ...... (laughs) ...... and I just sort of pulled my knickers across so he could see what I'd got and the teacher saw him but didn't see me and he got dragged out of his chair and I thought she was going to kill him! She was thumping his back and his bottom with her fist, you know. Course, I felt guilty about that as well. She didn't catch me! That was when I sort of started feeling great fear I suppose, you know, these adults have a huge potential to be so violent."

Some physical violence, especially in working class families, is considered 'normal' without any real understanding of the long-term effects on all concerned:

Linda: "I remember my brother being constantly spiteful and violent towards me so, that's a memory. We weren't very old so it wasn't, like, majorly serious, it wasn't like knives at my throat or anything but it was just like constant pain: arm up my back; leg twisted round; hand round my neck; just like, constant pain really – little bits of pain and him saying, 'Do you submit?' and I'd say, 'Yes! I submit!' straight away, 'I submit!' but he wouldn't stop. So, that would end up with me crying and that would always end up with my Dad getting hold of my brother and walloping him or taking him off somewhere and hitting him so that was that .... (cries). My brother doesn't have anyone now ... he's not in touch with anyone ... (cries)"

From infancy we are taught to be afraid of all strangers in case they molest us or abduct us; we are taught to be afraid of criminals who want to knock us down and steal our things or come into our houses at night and stab us in our beds; we are taught to be afraid of teachers at school who shout at us and may punish us or even beat us with canes:

Tim W: *"I got beaten at every single school that I went to! (laughs) I'm laughing but, you know, as a kid in the primary school I got, I remember, I'd broken my arm and there was a teacher called Miss Tucker who, unfortunately, knew a cousin of mine which was even worse. Because I was talking in class or something, she had me out at the front and she hit me with a ruler, the thin edge of the ruler, across my knuckles and I had one broken arm and the other arm held out while she whacked it with this ruler!"*

We are taught to be afraid not just of the adults, but also of school bullies who lie in wait for us in the toilet blocks or on the way home after school to beat us up:

Tim W: *"I remember, the most fearful memory was, I had been set upon as I was going through the school gates and I was only like about, I think I was about seven or eight, something like that, maybe and ever after then, I was terrified when it was the end of the day and*

I had to go home 'cos I had to go through these gates and run the gauntlet of these kids from the estate just up from where we lived who were gonna, you know, have a bit of fun!"

We are taught to be afraid of violent attacks because of our identities or skin colour. We are taught to be afraid of rival gangs with knives and vendettas. We are taught to be afraid of walking the streets in the dark in case of attack or rape, especially if we are female. We are taught to be afraid of crowds when trying to protest about things. We are taught to be afraid of our own police and armies when people start to organise against state repression. We are taught to be afraid of 'terrorists' who are living amongst us, secretly plotting to blow us up. We are taught to be afraid of other nations or political systems that would invade and take us over – destroying our way of life.

Some of us are even taught to be afraid of God who can see into our minds even when we have hidden ourselves under the pillow at night, knowing our innermost thoughts and punishing us for having the wrong ones.

Ultimately we are taught to be afraid of war and weapons of mass destruction – the nuclear holocaust which will end the world if we cannot threaten any potential aggressors with more deadly weapons of our own.

Like most feelings which have been created by hurtful experiences, they do not respond to evidence or logic. The facts and figures which show, for example, that it is much more likely that your child will be molested by someone in the family than a stranger in the park make no difference. We stop our children having fun running around outside just in case there is a dangerous weirdo hiding in the bushes, whilst happily leaving them with uncle 'touchy-feely' whilst we go out for the night.

STATE VIOLENCE

In Britain we are **not** taught to be afraid of the state and it's power over our lives – especially when we are young. In fact we are taught that the state is a benign 'nanny,' who looks after us when we need it, yet many of us experienced this power as a form of unrecognised violence:

Deuane: *"I've reflected on this ...... em ...... schooling actually ...... schooling, like you school a horse! ... One of the things I was picking up on then is, and this is violence really: one, I don't choose what I want to learn – someone else does that! I don't choose to follow my instincts. I don't choose to listen to someone who's in authority or not. I don't instinctively just leave and walk out and say, 'I'm off!' Basically, I've come to be quite a schooled animal, you know.... I suppose what I've come to be is someone who doesn't trust himself, you know, I don't trust myself because, I suppose, from that early schooling I've given my own authority and agency to the authorities and it's normal. A lot of time is taken by, I suppose, the state and whoever the experts were in charge of educational ideas and usually responding, I suppose, to business. Yeh man, taking the bloody piss! Fucking hell ...... yeh! The bloody cheek of it ...... telling me ...... then failing, you know ...... I didn't get my '11 plus' ..... and on and on and on!"*

Micheline: *"Violence. I mean, my memory is, my big feeling, my experience is that the State, the Health Service ... sort of feeling it owned me. That it had more power over me than my family did, you know, and could decide where I was to go, and my parents were scared to challenge them"*

Unless we get adequate opportunities to recover from these hurts we go through life living in fear of violence and we will run the serious risk of re-enacting that violence towards others whenever we see opportunities to hurt people who are smaller, physically less able to defend themselves and so on. Sometimes this can be extreme, yet remain hidden, especially within families:

Diana: *"What came into my head was my father abusing me when I was eleven months old. I thought I was drowning, I thought I was dying and the only thing I held onto was seeing the pear tree outside the window. Afterwards, I just didn't want to live and I refused to eat and I was in a bad state. That was the beginning really of the violence. And, like you said, all the lies! The lies, the layers and layers of lies – 'We are a happy family!' 'We are a happy family!' Everyone believed we were a happy family but I knew we weren't.*

"Now, I think there are two categories of people who make me feel violent: the people who remind me of my Dad and I have been violent to these people, really those men who sit on the tube like this (she spreads her knees wide apart) so, either you have to sit like this (squashed up) or you have to touch them and I went through a phase when travelling to work every morning on the underground when I'd get off and if they were staying on and it was crowded, as I walked out, with my big Doc Martins, I'd stomp on their feet and I'd be off the train and they'd be very surprised! But I've stopped doing it. I have stopped doing it. It wasn't as satisfying as one would wish! And I don't think they even understood why I did it!

"And the other thing is, when I'm in a situation that reminds me of being that child, in my insane family, who blamed everything that was wrong with the world on me – everything was my fault. So, often, my encounters with people who are in call centres or the NHS, where they tell you stuff that is clearly not right, is clearly bonkers, is clearly incorrect and you say, 'No, I don't think that's right!' and they insist it is and I just want to kill them! I wanna kill them!

"And I sometimes, I start behaving in a way ...... and then they're even worse ...... 'She's clearly a mad woman so we can treat her really badly'. It's completely counterproductive. It's very distressing. I don't know what the solution is!"

All the participants in our workshop on violence talked about their recognition that the perpetrators of the violence they had experienced had been victims of both personal and state violence themselves:

Linda: *"And it started for him because he had ...... he was abused by my Aunty when she was looking after him when he was very, very little and that's what triggered the whole thing".*

Alan: *"One of the things I learned just before my uncle died, which I never knew about him, was that, when my Dad's mother died, him and his sister were considered not old enough to look after themselves and they were put into children's homes. God knows, you know, what was going on there!"*

Diana: *"My Dad went to a public school when he was seven years old. He was brutalised there. I think this and the violence in the family is how we're conditioned to tolerate this economic thing. How the bosses learn to crush or they will be crushed."*

'HONOURABLE' VIOLENCE

The ultimate act of violence, killing another person, is something we still expect our young men to do in the name of patriotism or national defence but first we have to treat them with violence before they can do it. One prime example is in the methods used to take an ordinary man and turn him into a 'soldier'. Andy Loi, in a conversation on *TED* (a not-for-profit organisation that promotes 'Ideas Worth Spreading' - November 2012), speculated:

"What are the processes and strategies that the military use to alter the mind of a human being to become a soldier who is not afraid of taking another person's life? If you want people to kill other people, you have to make sure they see that 'the moral' is on their side – any soldier needs to be convinced that he and his comrades are 'the good guys' which, consequently, makes all the soldiers on the

other side the 'bad guys'. The whole nation needs to think this way. The vocabulary used usually contains words like freedom, human rights, humanity, innocent people, etc.

"Because the others are the 'bad guys' that makes the value of their lives already questionable. They may also kill woman, children and old people. They have no mercy, honor or anything else positive. They are the incarnation of EVIL!

"For soldiers in warfare, this 'black or white' concept is accompanied by a simple choice of either 'us' (me and my buddies) or 'them' which, in the face of enemy fire, is then pretty simple to make"

The US cavalry commander in the film *'Soldier Blue'* gave voice to the attitude he needed his recruits to take just prior to attacking a native village and butchering unarmed men, women and children:

"Think of it men, put into your minds the dark abominations of these Godless barbarians: murder, rape, torture and when you think of your comrades, fallen, butchered comrades, ask yourself, are we going to give them the same mercy – you just bet we are!"

An ex-soldier describes the process used to train new recruits for the US Military:

"Brutalization and desensitization are what happens at boot camp. From the moment you step off the bus you are physically and verbally abused: countless pushups, endless hours at attention or running with heavy loads, while carefully trained professionals take turns screaming at you. Your head is shaved, you are herded together naked and dressed alike, losing all individuality. This brutalization is designed to break down your existing mores and norms and to accept a new set of values that embrace destruction, violence, and death as a way of life. In the

end, you are desensitized to violence and accept it as a normal and essential survival skill in your brutal new world." From **'Trained to Kill', David Grossman 1998 (Illuminati News)**

And then we expect the same men to come home after military service and live a normal life again. The evidence is everywhere that this is almost impossible for many. For example, there have been more deaths through suicide of ex-soldiers than there were deaths through combat in the latest war in Afghanistan. There are many ex-combatants living on the streets who are homeless because they have not been able to recover from this brutalization and are therefore unable to feel 'safe' around even their families and loved ones. Others become secret abusers whilst trying to create a facade of normality:

Diana: *"My father was a barrister and all this time he was trying to become a Conservative MP and he was a young man in the war and went to war and when I was five I asked him how many people did he kill in the war and he reacted like (shouting) 'That is the most evil thing a little girl could ever ask her Daddy!' and I knew then, I knew, as a five-year-old, that that meant he'd killed lots of people".*

INTERNALISED VIOLENCE

It is impossible to escape being damaged to some degree by this system. It is really important that we don't fall into the trap of thinking that there are *good* people (us) and *bad* people (them). The only difference is our *personal history*. It will only be a difference in our stories that makes one person behave violently and compulsively and the rest of us able to not do something violent (even though we may think about doing it). A key part of that history will be the level of opportunity available to recover – the amount of attention there was around us from people who were able to listen to our stories and allow us to feel and express our hurts.

In response to the question 'What or who makes you feel violent?' it was clear to see in our workshops that, under a pleasant exterior, many of us are wrestling with all sorts of violent fantasies and urges, some of which occasionally get the better of us:

Micheline: "*Ian Duncan Smith! (Conservative Secretary of State for Work and Pensions) I find it very, very hard to see the warm, loving human being beneath the patterns! ...... (giggles) ...... Oh dear! I do imagine just pushing him over and maybe trampling on him a little bit! ...... Accidently running over his fingers! ...... Whoops, sorry! ...... Sorry about that tyre mark right across your face! ...... (giggles) ...... Oh dear, I really loath the man! More than I loath any of the others but I do loath the lot of them!... He's not a human being ...... He's an exception! ...... There are some you know – they come from outer-space! ...... they're masquerading as humans ... but they're not!*"

Tim W: "*Tories! That's a good start! ...... (laughs) ...... (shakes and shivers) ...... the most damaged people ...... going round accusing everybody else of being more damaged than them! ...... (shivers) ...... that's their raison d'etre isn't it! ...... but it's also the bloke that drove his car at me because I was cycling gently the wrong way up a one-way street the other day. He drove his car straight at me and I had to kind of, actually, get out of his way and then he put his fist on the horn five seconds before he got next to me! I know I was in the wrong but, you know, it's the violence in ..... what he's putting out, you know.*"

Micheline: "*It's important that you actually say what you want to do to these people!*"

Tim W: "*Well, I did think it would have been nice to pursue the guy in the car and then, like, when he came to a junction and had to stop, as he inevitably would in Richmond, I could get my keys out and key (scratch) his car, you know! That would have been quite satisfying! Or, just kicking the car, probably, would have been even more satisfying!*"

Linda: *"I mean, there are days when almost anyone who comes within my line of vision makes me feel angry – especially the people I love the most - apparently! So, there are times when I've been busy all day and I've just finished and I've just thought, 'I'll just have a few minutes on my own' and I'll hear Tim's key go in the front door and I think, 'Fucking Hell! What's he coming home for now?'*

"Apart from the people I love, who all infuriate the pants off me and make me want to swear at them – four-wheel-drive drivers – anyone really who drives a big car and insists on having the right-of-way when it's not their right-of-way, you know, 'cos they've got a big car so they just pull out in front of my little Micra – they just make me swear! I swear in the car so much! 'Fucking Wanker!' You know, this is the nice sort of exterior that I've perfected over the years of looking so calm, you know – it's all gone in the car really and in my head. Most of it takes place in my head! People tell me that they wouldn't know I was angry because I maintain this veneer of looking quite polite.

"And the other people that make me angry are - anyone who disses my children - in any shape or form! So, there was the man at the Festival Hall who I squirted the apple juice at, which was a bit of an impotent act of rage in a way but it felt satisfying at the time because he kept glaring at Maisie when she was very little while she was eating her crisps and Tim said to him, 'That tune was called, 'God Bless The Child!' and this bloke said, 'Great tune, horrible child!' and I said, 'Thurrrrrrr!' (squirts apple juice) – it just came out you know, thurrrrrrr, the apple juice! So, those categories: the people I love; the people that hurt my children and four-wheel-drive drivers – and politicians!"

Rose: *"Oh, there's so many things that make me angry - violent! I suppose, at the moment, it's my boyfriend, my partner who's alcoholic and I'm finding it quite hard. We've got it down to a reasonable level, well, what he thinks is a reasonable level! I think zero is a reasonable level! And, er, it just drives me mad!"*

Micheline: *"So, what would you like to do to him?"*

Rose: "*I just ... er ... scream at him! Just, 'STOP DRINKING!' and at the same time, I feel sort of contemptuous of other women who put up with it! ... (laughs) ... you know I think, 'Why do you put up with men like that?' And that's what I'm doing!'"*

Deuane: "*I suppose ...... people who are self-righteous, with opinions that are somehow the truth of all truths, you know. I suppose what I'd like to do to them, I'd just like to ... I don't want to beat them about the head with a lead pipe! I just wanna ... in the face of it, just to really express myself a bit really, rather than being quite measured and tempered and nice really. Just really express myself, you know, fully! I suppose I'm scared myself really.*"

Bev: "*I can be quite violent myself. My younger son, he's a bit like me, the way that I used to bait my mother and annoy my mother, he's now doing it to me! And I get really, really angry. I try to hold back with the anger and it's got violent where the police have been actually called. It's got so bad! For the last few months, since he's been working with his brother, it's much better. But, in the last few weeks he's been getting a bit upset, crying, saying he hates this whole system, doesn't wanna be here, hates this life, hates this ... hates the whole system, doesn't wanna be part of it, begging me to take him out of the school. "Get me a tutor!" Well, I can't afford a tutor! I can't afford to give up my job and so it's really hard. So, he's getting a bit upset. Then, last night, he was just baiting me and I just got up out of my chair and I went for him! I knew it would be alright 'cos my boyfriend was there so I knew, deep down, it would be alright because he wouldn't let me, you know, he wouldn't let me, these old feelings come up ... because when I was younger I was quite small and I got bullied sometimes and boys seemed to think they could do anything they wanted to me!*

"*I used to get really angry and violent. I always hit them or humiliated them verbally, you know and I think maybe it's bringing up issues to do with that. I think it is 'cos I was once carried out of a nightclub when a man tried to be rude to me. He tried to lift up my skirt and*

I went to punch him and I was the one they took me out of the night club! It was my fault! Fuck off! Stupid idiot!

"But he's bringing up things in me that I don't really like about myself but I'm just trying to own them. I'm reading a book called 'Facing Your Dark Side' – just looking at 'the things that annoy us in other people are sometimes the things about ourselves that we don't like'. And that's hard to acknowledge because sometimes it's true. The people that annoy me the most, make me really angry, well I wouldn't say make me 'cos I try to take ownership of my anger, I react to them in a way that I'm not happy with."

Alan: *"Sometimes in the car, I suppose that's my first thought. Usually when I'm by myself. I think I get angry when there's other people in the car with me but I tend not to do anything about it. I'm much more apt to have a go back at other people when I'm by myself. (laughs) There you go!"*

Micheline: *"What do you do, Alan, when you're by yourself?"*

Alan: *"It depends! Well, whatever needs doing!"*

Bev: *"What do you mean?"*

Rose: *"Give us an example."*

Alan: *"It doesn't usually involve any kind of collision!"*

Bev: *"What do you do?"*

Alan: *"Well, one example was, a guy who pissed me off once, I can't remember what he'd done but I was on a motorway and there were some road works approaching and the road works were down to one lane and I managed to maneuver myself so that I was just in front of him then I just slowed down – a lot! I crawled all the way through these road works. I don't know how far it was but he was going berserk behind me – I could see him the whole time! He was absolutely livid (laughs) but there was absolutely nothing he could do about it (laughs) and as soon as we got through, I just put my foot down and I was away! It was so sweet! He was going ballistic! (laughs) Oh dear!"*

Violence Works

As a tool of oppression and repression, violence works. Many of us can acknowledge the long-term effects on our ability to think and act powerfully when we are in situations which remind us of our early hurts:

Rose: "*I feel quite negative about human beings at the moment anyway with all the horrible things that have happened over the summer in the world and I'm finding it really hard to hang onto believing that human beings are fundamentally good. I think it doesn't take much to turn them into something really horrible and vicious people! I find that quite depressing really. It doesn't make for much hope for the future and I can just see the world going into a downward spiral somehow ...... I am a bit of a depressive anyway (laughs) so it doesn't take much to make me see all the bad in the world and there's a hell of a lot of bad at the moment.*"

Micheline: "*What do you think has happened to you to make you focus on the bad and to see that more than you see the good?*"

Rose: "*I suppose it's my childhood as well, you know, going to boarding school at a very young age and having my power taken away. I suppose it's left me quite helpless and powerless and that there's not a lot I can do about improving situations. I suppose most of my energies have gone into surviving my own life.*"

Bev: "*People I find it hard to relate to are: anyone in authority 'cos, of course, it reminds me of being a child again and being told what to do at school where I was kicked out of school at thirteen. I've had a problem with authority, I suppose, before that and that includes the police. I did have problems with the police... I looked out of the window of my dad's pub and I saw them basically man-handling a young woman – punching her in the stomach – and I was shocked because my parents brought me up to believe that the police were there to help you. You know, the local policeman was like the 'Big Ears' (the character in the 'Noddy' children's stories who was Noddy's*" *best friend), you know, and it was all kind of like that – like a little dream about how life should be."*

Linda: *"It's this thing where I don't feel I have any agency – that I can't do something which is going to make a difference.*

"The fact of our terms of employment for example, thinking about management, keeping it within the framework of my life: we don't have contracts; our contracts are temporary; there's no guarantee that we're going to have any hours next term or, you know, there's some talk of changing the contracts to three weeks – there's this exploitation of our labour and, at the same time, we're not paid very much and we're expected to put in a lot of extra work, preparation and so on and, at the same time, the college is advertising for managerial posts and they're £55,000 a year and, you know, free parking and blah, blah, blah and we can't park our cars!

"There's this divide, it's this shunting of me into this position where I don't count and what I say won't count and then me believing that… So, being in a meeting and feeling rattled and like I've got something to say but I can't say it because: 'Is that right? Is it true? Does anyone want to hear that? Am I just going to make a fool of myself?' … being afraid of being humiliated, afraid of being put down, afraid of, you know, loosing whatever job I've got… being publicly scuppered – shown to be the idiot that I am, shown to be ignorant, shown to not know anything about anyone, you know and not to have read enough papers all my life or, you know, anything: the fear of humiliation; the fear of being embarrassed; the fear of being publicly shamed.

"Shame is a big feature in this. I seem to have a ridiculously large burden of shame about the smallest things and it's something I want to do to other people, you know: 'Who did that? Who was it that left the fridge door open?' You know, 'Who did this? Who left the light on last night?' You know, this great desire to find …… and target. So, I'm expecting – that's a two-way street isn't it – I expect that to come back at me"

Micheline: *"So, where did the shame come from?"*

Linda: "*My mother. Mostly my Mum and, to a lesser extent, my Dad, (almost whispered) 'Oh, you are hopeless! You can't do this! Oh …!' And, I suspect, other adults in the family. It's from childhood! It's a childhood thing. And teachers and Miss Page at school who was this gimlet-eyed, dried-up old bag, you know, who …… So, where's their humanity? See, I can't … (laughs) … I can't find a human in her! … the worst aspect of that disempowerment is that it takes away your internal motivation so that all your motivation becomes about pleasing other people, getting it right for other people, rather than finding out, from inside, you know, always looking to have the motivation from outside. I think that's the most disempowering thing and that's like societal – it comes with oppression*".

Deuane offered perhaps the best illustration of how oppression is most debilitating in its internalised form:

Deaune: "*I remember when I was about nine years old, in primary school and a new girl came in and, looking back, I suspect she was maybe in care or something like that 'cos she appeared in the middle of a term. Short hair, looked … I guess I would've had a reason but she looked different. I think, looking back, she probably looked poor, so she was different and I, you know, I was just a normal guy but I just started like really being unpleasant to her, you know, like teasing her and nasty – bullying I suppose! It just came out of me! Where the hell did that come from?*"

Micheline: "*What had you learned about poor kids?*"

Deaune: "*It was just something 'not good!' Not good, just 'not good!' I don't know what it was. It was just irrational and maybe it was like, 'You're different, you're different!' You know, 'Attack!' 'Get away!' *"

Micheline: "*Do you remember how you learned that it was not good to be poor?*"

Deaune: "*Your question actually said, 'Why did I behave like that* to that girl?' and it was because she looked poor and actually, I realise, we were a poor family so it was actually, who knows, me projecting, seeing, 'I hate you! You're disgusting! You're a looser! You're different! You're outside! You need punishing!' and it's kind of what – reflecting on the workshop – how much of my self oppression is internalised, you know. I'm actually under control – controlled by me now! Don't need any force doing anything, you know! The leash is off, the gates are down, the fence is off but I ain't going anywhere, you know!"

Linda: "You can see how this structure keeps the ignorance, the reactionary view of the world, the anti-life, the anti-joy, the anti-love if you like, feeling about keeping people and things in their place in order to carry on this terrible confusion and this terrible misunderstanding which, at better moments, all human beings shrug off, you know, willingly."

LOVE, THE NATURAL WAY HUMANS FEEL ABOUT EACH OTHER

"The concepts of love and power are usually contrasted as polar opposites. Love is identified with a resignation of power and power with a denial of love. What is needed is a realisation that power without love is reckless and abusive and love without power is sentimental and anaemic. Power, at its best, is love implementing the demands of justice." **Martin Luther King Jr.**

"Love is the only sane and satisfactory answer to the problem of human existence" **Erich Fromm**

Love is all around us but we don't notice it. We don't notice it because our attention is directed towards protecting ourselves from the threatened violence (mentioned above) or all the other things we have described in the previous chapters.

Bev's Poem *(excerpt)*

I pluck a word
I pin it to the page
Together, my heart, my emotions, my imagination, my desire,
All come together to form an idea manifest
Birds sing their life's story.
I hear them.
Living now, they offer freedom.
The wind blows, the trees dance.
Life is here.
A life, yet, unseen.
We look outside for beauty,
Never realising that it's within...

The media fuel these fears every day with gruesome stories of attacks on helpless people. They do not of course report the millions of stories of people coming to each other's aid, treating each other kindly, protecting each other from danger or simply going out into the world and enjoying life which is not news, because it is the normal everyday experience of most people.

We are not talking here about the red-hearted sentimental version of love in valentine cards or Hollywood films but of the real kind, which motivates most of us to do all that unpaid and unrecognised labour every day of our lives: cooking; cleaning and caring for each other. It is also the main motive to do most of the work within the public sector and the voluntary sector which, between them, account for a huge percentage of the labour force.

Much of this work is almost invisible unless you happen to be an employee or 'user' of the service. One example is the thousands of home carers employed by local authorities to wash, dress, tidy up and provide meals for a multitude of elderly, ill or disabled people who have no one else to do it for them.

I (Micheline) have been supported by this service myself and I have seen them support many others, often without much appreciation.

I remember particularly an elderly, sick and alcoholic neighbour of mine who did nothing but curse and yell at the pairs of women who came to attend to him three times a day. His unpleasant voice permeated my flat which was directly below his, making me wonder how these workers could put up with it day after day. But when I asked them, they said something like 'Oh the poor man can't help it' and then went on to tell me how worried they were that his doctor wasn't visiting him enough, their eyes full of concern. Many of these carers were not born in Britain but in countries where it was unheard of to leave elderly parents to fend for themselves. They felt it was their duty to fill this 'love gap' and they did.

Many necessary jobs are not 'nice' and it can be quite a puzzle to understand why people do them for those who believe money and status are the only things which matter. A recent television series followed the working lives of a group of men employed by a large water authority (*The Watermen, 'A Dirty Business'*, BBC Two, 2014). Their jobs involved the kind of tasks many people believe no one would do unless they were desperate for work – sloshing about in stinking sewage and creeping around underground tunnels full of rats. But the men themselves said, once they got used to the smells, that they loved their work. A clue to why this might be came after one long day answering emergency calls to unblock people's drains of clogged up mangles of baby wipes and disposable nappies. As one bloke threw his tools in the back of their van and locked up for the night, he made a remark, thrown with a grin to the camera – 'Another day saving the world!' It was spoken with a tone of satisfaction that you rarely hear from any of the suited people pouring out of their offices of an evening after a hard day at the photocopier or board meeting.

Public sector jobs in Britain were created, for the most part, in the post-World War Two era when the country felt that everyone who had joined in the war effort now deserved a decent life with a universal system of sufficient social housing, healthcare, education, public services, State Pensions, Child Allowances and Social Security – all paid for collectively. The incoming Labour government, led by Clem Attlee, said it was the first government voted in by the people 'under a socialist ticket'. You could say this was a system based on love or altruism but, right from the start, it was seen as a danger by those who wished to defend and expand private ownership and the accumulation of wealth in the hands of an elite. We are now fighting hard to prevent these jobs being transferred to the private sector where the profit motive dominates and 'love' has nothing to do with the provision of services.

Even those public sector jobs which still exist are becoming progressively de-humanised and unsatisfying. Extraordinary rules emanate from the Health and Safety Executive or the Child Protection Policies outlawing the hugging of small children who have fallen over in the play ground or lifting a disabled child out of their wheelchair so they can play with their friends in the sandpit. This is mostly not to do with protecting employees or children from harm but with protecting employers from the fear of costly litigation,

Employees of churches too can play a big part in trying to remind us that we are spiritual beings with bigger goals to think about than the size of our bank balances. There are many thousands of paid priests and vicars, imams and rabbis, Quakers and Buddhists and other religious leaders with their followers, and voluntary workers providing all sorts of activities and services from food banks to 'Alcoholics Anonymous'. They help bind communities together by offering opportunities for believers to gather together, to reflect, to refocus on deeper issues, to be guided, to be forgiven, to channel loving thought to others through prayer. All the major religions share a doctrine of altruism at their core, and many members of faith communities admit that their religious teachings are not the cause of the many appalling things which are done in their name but rather in the inability of people to actually follow their faith.

'Love' is hard to define, but we know it when we see it or feel it. It is in the little things – ironing your grandma's hankies, feeding the birds in your garden, taking a lost wallet to the police station, making your partner a cup of tea in bed, doing shopping for an elderly neighbour, listening to someone who is upset until they can think clearly again. It is in the middle sized things – adopting or fostering other people's children, donating an organ to a stranger when you die and it is in the big things – jumping into freezing cold water or running into burning buildings, risking your life, to save a complete stranger who is in trouble. Over and over we hear such people dismissing their acts as just 'Doing what *anyone* would do'.

In the world we have currently created, there do not seem to be enough opportunities to express our love. Apart from the highly charged narrow channel of sexual relationships and possibly our immediate families, if we are lucky, we have to search around for places to let these feelings flow. Our pets get a lot of the over-spill in Britain in particular – especially dogs and cats. Children often direct a lot of love at their toys, stuffed animals and dolls. Actors in TV soaps get an astounding amount of presents or birthday cards from their viewers who confuse their roles with reality.

If we noticed this need to love we would start to feel very differently about ourselves and the world but this instinct is a problem to the proponents of capitalism. They need us to feel bad about ourselves and each other and constantly dissatisfied with what we have, in order to keep the wheels of commerce turning. Consequently there is much force used in persuading us to over-ride our inherent caring for each other.

In my early life (Micheline) back in the 1950s, when a disabled baby like me was born, it was common practice in hospitals to not allow the parents to see or touch their baby to prevent them 'bonding'. Instead, they would be told that their baby was a 'dud' and they should leave her or him behind in the hospital. 'Forget about this child and go and have another' they would be advised, knowing that only complete separation could stop the love relationship forming. Some parents did and some, like mine, didn't but the professionals concerned often saw their acts of defiance as incomprehensible. 'How could you have so much love for a child like that?'

Sadly, this attitude has not entirely gone away. Disabled people are not generally considered able to be productive and are therefore still considered only as burdens to society. Our parents' love, in fact, is sometimes the only thing which saves and continues our lives.

Who will win? Or rather, which part of our nature will come to dominate future societies and systems? Violence is always a reflection of our hurts. Love however isn't something you can demand of people, nor is it productive to simply exhort people to act in more loving ways. This only leads to pretence. The task is rather to uncover our loving core. By allowing us first to bring into consciousness layers of hurt which have created feelings which are not natural to us but which have been left as 'battle scars' from the past, obscuring our real nature and then, in a situation of relative safety, in which you know you will not be attacked or judged for having such feelings, a natural healing process can start to operate. Through the talking, giggling, weeping and sometimes storming, old rigidities can be dissolved into simple memories which no longer drive our behaviour. Little bit by little bit we become more authentic, more real – more human. Our intelligence has more space in which to operate. We are more able to act towards the common good. Our love shines through:

> *"When you are in conflict or doubt, or afraid, when you lose hope, or lose people that you depend on, move beyond the pain and fear, there is an awareness there. In your loneliness and suffering and darkness and fear, silently behind it, the awareness is waiting for us to return. This awareness is the field of conciousness from which all life came, the absolute energy that precedes all and is beyond all and is within all. It is within you.*

We all have this in common but we have been convinced that we are alone, but this energy which compels one cell to become two, that heals wounds, that spins quarks and planets, is within us all. And all language can do is rest on top of it, or point to it, never really describing it, this force, this undeniable compulsion to come together, we all know that it's there and we all know when it is absent and we all know that we must be open to it now. And in spite of its ethereal and indefinable nature, we all know that it is love". **Russell Brand, 'Revolution'**

Section Three

CONCLUSION

There can no longer be a question about the need to think again about how we humans organise ourselves. Danny Dorling, Professor of Geography at Oxford University, recently set out the stark reality before us. He has suggested that as capitalism steadily moves the wealth ever upwards into the hands of 1% of the world's population, the proportion they own will soon be 100%, along with all the power and control that goes with it. This could trigger an economic collapse on a monumental scale, and bring with it all the dangers of people panicking with their fingers on the nuclear button. Naomi Klein in her book *'This Changes Everything: Capitalism Vs the Climate'* pinpoints our economic system as the underlying driver for climate change, and reinforces the conclusion that we must replace it with something new – the 'next' economy – if we are to survive as a species.

We are the one species on this planet with the power to destroy it, and conversely with the power to plan for our continued existence in ways which lead to a more fair, equal and sustainable future for us all.

We set out in this joint enterprise to see if we could find ways to help interested people to shed light on a baffling experience common to us all – seeing that we don't always act in ways which relate to our best thinking, but get drawn into all manner of less helpful behaviours instead – behaviours which often sabotage our own plans and dreams.

We had no intention of writing a guide for 'A Quick Fix For Irrationality' (try the online *'Cognitive Behaviour Therapy'*, favoured by our current government for that, as it will apparently help you to overcome all your problems in just eight weeks, mostly so you can get back to work instead of wallowing in misery at the tax-payers expense). We know that what we are proposing is only one of many things we need to be doing long-term to truly transform the ways we live with each other. We feel, however, that what we could achieve is to help see human behaviour, including our own, in a new light. If we better understood the phenomena of the human distress pattern and its ability to 'restimulate' us (trigger repetitive responses relating to painful experiences from our past), then we could approach any new human situation from a new point of view, with new strategies and new solutions designed to accurately fit the current reality resulting in helpful, humane and sustainable outcomes. We could know for example that we don't have to hate anyone, just their 'patterns', and we could believe that all humans are doing the best that their circumstances allow – including ourselves. We could reserve our hatred for the systems that result in this 'patterned' behaviour and go to war with them rather than with each other.

This is not some liberal, wishy-washy, just-be-nice-to-everyone sort of mantra. Our patterns can be extremely destructive and need to be acknowledged as such, especially the fact that they do not respond to a reasoned argument or being faced with the 'facts' (think UKIP!). They need to be managed, and sometimes that even means locking the person who is being controlled by such patterns away from harm's way. The difference is separating these patterns in our minds from the human they have colonised, and fighting to rescue the person behind them or, better still, creating the conditions under which such patterns would not be installed in the first place.

We hope that reading the book alone may help you find this new understanding. However, we feel also that being able to turn this understanding into action might need more support.

Capitalism could be likened to a house of cards. The whole structure is held together by different components which are all essential to its continuation. If we took out any one of these components the whole edifice would collapse. Our study has concentrated on seven of these components, beginning with 'isolation'. We began with this because we believe this is the one which prevents us tackling all the others, but is also the easiest to 'undo'.

We saw that drawing together people for a few hours in a private venue, and allowing them to answer questions in a structured format seemed to help people to connect:

Will: "It's an experience which isn't done enough. I can really see the value of being listened to. You are not using your mind to try and interpret what people are saying, so you are leaving yourself open to really hearing them. All of us shared pain - shared wounds. It is what connects all of us. It's good to be vulnerable."

Tim B: "I found it fascinating listening. I enjoyed being listened to seriously by Joe. I realised how very everyday 'trivial' events can have a very powerful effect when you are a child. Events can wound and be momentous and I thought you could only be a healer if you have acknowledged your own wounds. It was a good experience for me because I usually find other people want to do all the talking so one doesn't have a chance. My wife and I have just been on holiday with another couple and at the end my wife and I were both exhausted because they talked non-stop. It was interesting but exhausting just listening."

Joe: "It was lovely. Something came into my head that happened and I hadn't known what to do with it but Tim made it incredibly easy to be able to sort of express that, to put words to it, and also to find myself feeling pretty angry and having that experience made it much easier for me to listen without wanting to comment. It was very safe. I felt very comfortable and I could have been with you on that holiday and bored you to death with all I had to say but it was a lovely six minutes."

Ayana: "That was a treat, was to hear about other people's experiences and to hear how important the parents' role is in all this - how they bring up their children and the balance they hold. How important it is to a child

- the decisions you make. And I am sure I'm going to continue thinking about it when I go home and in the next days to come."

Susan: *"What do you really need in your life? I thought that it was really good to think about that."*

Pandora: *"The system worked really well for me... in the beginning I had a lot to say 'cos it's that kind of personal experience stuff that we all know quite well then, the questions at the end I perceived as harder but still absolutely fine to talk about it for a bit in such a safe space that was created. So, really good!"*

Ben: *"I'm glad that I showed up for this. It's been a bit hard work for me because I'm really tired and hung-over, talking about young people and patterns and what not. But also because it's big stuff that we're talking about so it would feel heavy without a headache. As for the structure, I found it totally relaxing when you explained the structure and time bit and it was like, "OK, there's a format, there's a method here". That does make it safe - for me. It's been really nice to hear what everyone else had to say as well. We never take the time to listen to each other like this and it's always really special when we do, so thanks."*

Lucy: *"I've really enjoyed hearing people's thinking actually. It's an interesting topic to think about generally. It's sort of everything. It's a massive topic."*

Jennifer S: *"It was good having that attention to talk and knowing that it didn't matter if I stopped, yawned or did what I wanted, they would still have their attention on me. There was no pressure to get information out there. I hope I gave them the same sort of experience to talk freely."*

Dania: *"Initially, I thought three minutes was a very short time but I was quite surprised at the end of six minutes that I realised how language can be used as a barrier. It can become competitive but it can also be a way in which I shield my vulnerability because I can use language in that way. I have never been in this situation before. It is through meetings like this that we can keep an eye on the system and I liked that a lot. It is not professional but intensely personal so there was no formality – no pretence."*

Will: *"I think that our discussions are with a vocabulary that is close to our core - about things I really care about."*

Beth: *"I really got a lot out of it. I am trying to challenge myself to do more thinking about things at the moment and particularly something as personal as that workshop, I think really pushed up against what I would have done 'normally' but in a really supportive and comfortable atmosphere. It also makes me think about how I can be in more practical meetings where I feel very confident and how I could have an effect on other people's feelings of being able to contribute."*

Jerry: *"It was interesting for me because my comfort zone is listening. I like listening. I enjoy that - putting my attention there for others. So, having the attention on me, usually I'm used to that one-to-one, so opening myself up about different things, whether I'm knowledgeable on certain subjects or not, 'cos I feel safe, you know, that was nice. It was an opportunity to share and to learn which I felt I did both, so I'm grateful for that."*

Pandora: *"Imagine if school was like that!"*

We assume that if it was done more than once, so the group could build its safety and have more time to work, these workshops would be even more useful. We have included therefore an appendix which is a template for running listening groups such as those described above. They need to be free of charge, and led by a volunteer who has experience of running groups, 'holding' the safety and making sure everyone participates.

Our next exploration will be to find ways to help train and support facilitators who may not yet have the confidence to lead such a group. If you are interested in exploring this idea with us, please contact us through our website: www.healingthehurtsofcapitalism.com or emailing us at: mich@michathome.wanadoo.co.uk or alansprung@care4free.net

Only you readers can tell us if we succeeded.

APPENDIX

GUIDELINES FOR 'HEALING THE HURTS' SUPPORT GROUP LEADERS

A 'Healing the Hurts' support group is based on the understanding that we all need a safe space in our lives in which we can think and feel without fear of criticism or judgement. When we experience the undivided attention of one or more people our natural emotional healing processes automatically start to work.

We may talk about things which have upset us, or a problem we need to solve, or we may focus on a specific question asked by the group's convenor. Sometimes emotions may rise up and we will cry, or laugh, or yawn whilst we are talking. All this helps clear our minds of distress which has built up inside us, weighing us down or confusing us. We come away feeling lighter and more able to think about our situation. Because we have also listened to other people, we often feel less isolated and more connected with others and this makes us stronger.

When we do this regularly, the safety will build up and we will find it more and more useful. Although this sounds simple, the safety will only happen within a very tight structure and agreed-upon ground rules. The groups must be led by someone who will create this structure and make sure the ground rules are kept.

THE GROUND RULES

Confidentiality: what is said in each person's time is completely confidential. No one refers to it again, even in their time, except the person themselves.

Everyone has an equal amount of time during which no one

interrupts or comments on what they are saying, but maintains an attitude of respect, interest and delight.

The expression of emotion is welcomed and even encouraged. It must not be confused with the painful events from which the person is trying to recover. Conversely, it should not be expected that everyone will have the same degree of access to their emotions, especially at first. Talking freely is in itself very useful.

CREATING THE STRUCTURE

- Invite between four – eight people you like to join you in a 'Healing the Hurts' support group.

- Decide on a time and a place which suits you all. The place must be private, and is usually someone's home. You need to meet for at least fifteen minutes per person (the bigger the group the longer you will need).

- Encourage people to be punctual.

- You may or may not offer refreshments before or after the group.

- Make an agreement every time you meet that the things shared in the group remain confidential to the person who said them, are not commented upon by other members of the group or ever referred to again (other than by the person who said them, if they wish).

- Sit in a circle as close as you can. If you are comfortable with it, holding hands will add to the safety for everyone.

- Go round the group and ask everyone to say something that has gone well lately, or something they are pleased with. Share their pleasure but do not start a conversation about it.

- Divide the remaining time up equally between the numbers of people present, leaving about 10 minutes for a closing circle.

- When these groups are starting up and people are not used to using this kind of attention, it can be very useful for the convenor to ask a question for everyone to answer in turn. **This question must require an answer which is personal, not general**. For example it will not work to ask "What do you think are the problems with capitalism?" or "Is competition a good thing?" The question must be along the lines of "What impact has capitalism had on your life?" or "What was your earliest memory of competition?"

- Set a timer and go round the circle giving your undivided attention to each person in turn. They can use their time to talk about anything they want if they are too preoccupied to answer the initial question. The leader may ask individuals further questions to encourage the person to say more, or to allow themselves to feel the feelings that they have been holding in, e.g. "How did that feel?" Have a box of tissues available for those who need them.

- The leader also takes a turn and is a 'peer', not an 'expert.'

- For the last ten minutes let each person take a turn to say something they are looking forward to doing in the near future. Say farewell and remind people of the next meeting and make sure people say if they are unable to come.

You may want to follow this with a bit of less structured time, but it is not necessary, and may tempt people to forget the confidentiality agreement whilst chatting over a piece of banana cake.

Once set up, do not invite new people to join without consulting the whole group.

No one is responsible for anyone else in the group, however 'desperate' they may appear. The purpose of these groups is to empower each person to take control of their own lives, and to bring about the changes they need. Our confidence that we can do this is part of what will make the group work.

Holding hands and hello/goodbye hugs are very helpful, but not to be forced on people.

Further Reading

A small selection of books and videos which helped inform this book:

Baird V. and Ransom D. *People First Economics*

New Internationalist Publications 2010

A collection of short essays by radical thinkers, including Noam Chomsky, Susan George and Naomi Klein. Evo Morales promotes his 10 step program to save the world, life and humanity in this very readable, informative and inspiring publication.

Fromm E. *To Have or To Be?*

Continuum Publishing Group 2005

A psychologist and socialist, Erich Fromm discusses the effects of materialism on our well-being, proposing that dependence on outside 'things' for our sense of self would lead to deep seated insecurity rather than fulfilment.

See also 'The Art of Loving', 'Escape From Freedom' and 'The Sane Society'. All also available as audiobooks.

Jackins H. *The Human Side of Human Beings*

Rational Island Publications
(Order through www.rc.org)

Written over 60 years ago this book is still unique in its proposition about the source of human irrationality. Having accidentally discovered that crying with someone's attention seemed to help the distressed person to be able to think more clearly, and to consequently act more effectively, Jackins set up experimental sessions and workshops to develop what became the theory and practice of Re-evaluation Counseling. After twenty years this was the first book to set out in detail the evidence from this body of work. It suggested our real nature was obscured by the distorting effects of our oppression(s) rather than by 'disease' and as such offers a different solution to the problems which face us.

JAMES O. AFFLUENZA: *THE ALL CONSUMING EPIDEMIC*.

EBURY PRESS 2007

Based on a hypothesis by the author, a psychologist, that capitalism has infected us with a 'virus' which drives us to seek affluence and status without bringing any further happiness, this book is full of insightful interviews with people of all levels of income including the super-rich. It constitutes a very important challenge to the idea that there are any real winners under our current system.

JONES O. : *CHAVS – THE DEMONISING OF THE WORKING CLASS*

VERSO BOOKS (PAPERBACK) APRIL 2010.

A powerful book written at a time of increasing inequality driven by the owning classes as they try to defend their elitism by blaming the poor for their poverty. Jones describes how the working class in Britain have had their self-worth systematically attacked, their traditional work shipped abroad where labour is cheaper, their unions denigrated and disempowered, their proud histories hidden, their needs for housing and other services not met, and their economic safety-net withdrawn. At the same time, the media have relentlessly put forward stereotypes of working class people as scroungers, unwilling to work and living off others because of personal failings. From this perspective it is easier to understand their anger even if sometimes misdirected at each other.

See also 'The Establishment And How They Get Away With It' by the same author.

KLEIN N. *THIS CHANGES EVERYTHING: CAPITALISM VERSUS THE CLIMATE.*

SIMON AND SCHUSTER 2014

"Klein exposes the myths that are clouding the climate debate. We have been told the market will save us, when in fact the addiction to profit and growth is digging us in deeper every day. We have been told it's impossible to get off fossil fuels when in fact we know exactly how to do it—it just requires breaking every rule in the "free-market" playbook: reining in corporate power, rebuilding local economies, and reclaiming our democracies.

We have also been told that humanity is too greedy and selfish to rise to this challenge. In fact, all around the world, the fight for the next economy and against reckless extraction is already succeeding in ways both surprising and inspiring." Read more and watch the excellent video on the book website: www.thischangeseverything.org

LEONARD A. *THE STORY OF STUFF – HOW OUR OBSESSION WITH STUFF IS TRASHING THE PLANET, OUR COMMUNITIES AND OUR HEALTH – AND A VISION FOR CHANGE.*

CONSTABLE & ROBINSON LTD. 2010

A young American teacher describes her own journey of discovery, and shock, as she sought to learn how things are made and the devastating impact of their production on the people who make them, buy them and on the planet itself. A very popular animated twenty minute film summary of the book is available to view on You Tube. Watch also her 'Story of Change'.

PIKETTY T. *CAPITAL IN THE 21ST CENTURY*

HARVARD UNIVERSITY PRESS 2014

This is not an easy read but it has reached the consciences of people thinking about economy across the political spectrum. Piketty, an economist himself, explains in detail why the 'trickle down effect' is a myth and how those with money tend to make more money.

To read an excellent summary and critique of this book by Stuart Watkins go to www.leftunity.org and search for An Introduction to Thomas Piketty's 'Capital in the 21st Century'

TRESSEL R. *THE RAGGED TROUSERED PHILANTHROPISTS*

FIRST PUBLISHED 1914. LATEST EDITION HARPER COLLINS

This book was written in story form to help working people understand how their labour makes the rich richer whilst they themselves continually struggle to survive. It is one of the most accessible books on the subject of capitalism and has been in print for over 100 years. The chapter called 'The Great Money Trick' is essential reading. An underfunded but nevertheless excellent short film made by the sixteen year old George Moore which dramatises this chapter is available on You Tube: The Ragged Trousered Philanthropists, George Moore Films.

Robert Tressell himself did not live to see his book published or to know the huge help it would be to our struggle for a classless society.

WILKINSON R. AND PICKETT K.: *THE SPIRIT LEVEL – WHY EQUALITY IS BETTER FOR EVERYBODY*

PENGUİN 2010

A collection of statistics painstakingly gathered in the 'developed' world which illustrates beyond doubt the direct relationship between economic inequality and social problems of all kinds. The popularity of the book led to the formation of the Equalities Trust: www. equalitytrust.org.uk with many local campaigning groups now formed. They are making a film with crowd funding to take the findings of the book to a larger audience. This will be launched in 2015. To see a trailer go to www.thespiritleveldocumentary.com

Thanks and Acknowledgements

Many thanks to all the people who participated in the workshops and made comments and suggestions for the final version of this book:

Des Sowerby, Will Parkinson, Ella Sprung, Jennifer Dine, David Towell, Zelda McCollum, Tara Flood, Joe Whittaker, Jennifer Smith, Beth Ash, Dania Thomas, Tim Brooke, Ayana Teklemariam, Susan Harris, Christine Wilson, Jill and John Miller, Carrie Mogford, Tim Kahn, Beverley Alfred, Deuane Germon, 'Rose', Lucy Mason, Pandora Jane, Ben Feder, Gerry, 'Diana', Linda and Tim Whitehead.

Thanks to Tim Kahn and Maggie Holdsworth for careful proof reading and many useful comments and suggestions.

We would especially like to acknowledge the thinking of the late Harvey Jackins (1916–1999) and the many other colleagues around the world (including each other) who helped develop and refine the body of theory and practice called 'Re-evaluation Counseling' from which we have derived much of our capacity to write this book.

We hope it will help to justify Harvey's belief that we humans have the power within us to make whatever kind of world we want.

ABOUT THE AUTHORS

Alan Sprung attended his local primary schools on the council estate in Coventry where he grew up and later went to Caludon Castle School, a large boys comprehensive, until he was 16 years old and on to Henley College of Further Education for one year. In 1967 he embarked on an engineering technician apprenticeship with AEI where he learned many engineering skills and helped to produce fractional horsepower motors and switchgear for the aircraft industry.

Alan has had many different paid jobs over the years including: Workshop Technician in a secondary school; Labourer on the nightshift in a Chrysler car factory; Community Photographer; CNC Lathe – Programmer, Setter, Operator; Project Worker / Trainer based at Coventry Peace House and he most recently worked in Birmingham as a Support Worker with a young man whose life is challenged by autism and epilepsy.

Alan's 'political' education was gleaned from: his father, Jack Sprung, a life-long socialist, trade unionist and political activist; from his involvement with the Woodcraft Folk when he was young; from all of his own work experiences; from his activities as a Union Representative within local government; from his involvement with the Re-evaluation Counselling Community and from his work with refugees and asylum seekers at Coventry Peace House.

Alan is a photographer, songwriter, musician and a keen skier and mountain walker.

Micheline Mason is an artist, writer, activist and campaigner. She was born in London in 1950, to a father 'raised poor' in England, and a mother 'raised poor' in Mauritius. Micheline attended art college before becoming involved with the Women's Movement. As a disabled person, Micheline has been at the forefront of the Disability Rights Movement and a leader within the Inclusion Movement since the early 1980's. She is best known for her work campaigning for inclusive education and equality in schools. More recently, Micheline has been dedicated to campaigning against the Government's austerity measures. She is the author of several books and many articles. In her retirement Micheline is also a parent, writer, painter and poet. She has recently (2015) been elected to be a Principle Speaker with Left Unity, a new political party which aims to help move us towards the next economy whilst safeguarding the most vulnerable members of society from the harmful effects of capitalism. She lives in London and loves watching birds and tending her garden.

Index